GODS AND GAMES

GODS
AND
GAMES *toward a theology of play*

David L. Miller

The World Publishing Company
New York and Cleveland

PERMISSIONS

Acknowledgment is gratefully made to the following for permission to quote from
the sources indicated.

AMERICAN ASSOCIATION OF UNIVERSITY PROFESSORS
    From "The Humanities, The Whore, and The Alderman" by Douglas J. Stew-
art. Copyright 1965. *AAUP Bulletin*, LI, 1 (Autumn, 1965).
APPLETON-CENTURY-CROFTS
    From *The Madness in Sports* by Arnold R. Beisser. Copyright 1967. Used by
permission.
BEACON PRESS
    From *Eros and Civilization* by Herbert Marcuse. Copyright 1955, © 1966
by Beacon Press. Reprinted by permission of the Beacon Press.
DELACORTE PRESS and GEORGE ALLEN & UNWIN LTD.
    From *The Master Game* by Robert S. DeRopp. Copyright © 1968 by Robert
S. DeRopp. A Seymour Lawrence Book/Delacorte Press. Used by permission.

The following page constitutes a continuation of the copyright page.

TO DONNA, a playmate

Acknowledgments

I very much wish to acknowledge my debt of gratitude to the
following persons for the role they have played in bringing this
book into print: to Professor Gabriel Vahanian, whose idea it was
originally that The World Publishing Company and I come together
on this project; to Professor Stanley R. Hopper, in whose graduate seminars, many years ago, ideas were conceived which were
later to come to this fruition; to Mr. Ted Estess, Mr. Carl Eller-
man, Miss Joyce Flood, Miss Janet Bralove, and Miss Sandra
Browning, the student assistants who labored long hours in various phases of research, bibliography, and manuscript preparation;
to Professor James B. Wiggins, a colleague whose collegiality in
discussion served as midwife, nursing to life many of these ideas;
and to my wife, who suffered most the year's labor of this book's
birth. It is to her, therefore, that this book is dedicated.

DAVID L. MILLER

Contents

Part Three PLAY'S MYTHOLOGY

INTRODUCTION

"The Care and Feeding of Hobby Horses"

Two Significant Events, or The Recent Beginnings of Ideas about Play In 1934 Earnest Elmo Calkins wrote a book called *The Care and Feeding of Hobby Horses*. It was published by the Leisure League of America and contained seven hundred suggestions for the use of leisure time as well as a bibliography of fifteen hundred books on hobbies and sports. Two thousand and two hundred odd ways to have, as the writer put it, "keen delight"! "How many are there," Calkins asked, "who can tie a square knot? Why should not more of us know how to make a splice, or a hitch, or a tackle? Why do we not learn the simple laws of mechanics that apply to the things around us, that we use daily? Greater manual dexterity would reduce the friction of living. . . ."[1] And so on and on he wrote.

Calkins was serious, of course. That may have been his book's greatest deficiency: overseriousness and overzealousness about play. But one other deficiency must be noted, also. Neither in the fifteen-hundred-item bibliography nor in the text of the book was reference made to what has come to be a most significant event in the recent history of ideas. The event had occurred the year before Calkins' book was published. The rector of Leyden University in Holland took for the topic of his annual lecture a subject he had been at work on for some thirty years. The topic was: "The Cultural Limits of Play and the Serious." This lecture was expanded to book form in 1938, at which time Johan Huizinga's *Homo Ludens* became the firm base for a most startling revolution in human meaning. It became the metaphor of—dare we say it?—a new mythology whose components in the world of ideas are game-theory and play-theory.

Huizinga was serious, too, of course. But in a way different from Calkins. Calkins' book is serious about everyday life, about reducing "the friction of living." Huizinga, on the other hand, is serious about ideas, about the idea of play which, if properly possessed by the human imagination, may well lead to a playfulness about "the friction of living."

By Word of Mouse: A Parable about This Book   The difference between Calkins and Huizinga may be demonstrated through a parable about the joy of life's frictions. The time of the parable is thirty-three years after Huizinga's address and Calkins' book. It is December, at a winter resort in the Pennsylvania Poconos. Four young university professors—a sociologist, a philosopher, a theologian, and an instructional technologist—are seated at lunch with their wives. The conversation has been lively and nonserious. The philosopher's wife has been jesting with the theologian about the latter's apparent disregard for fact and his apparent obsession with fantasy. And now this same woman tells a story, for no apparent reason.

"This is true. It was told to me as a fact," she alleges, and then goes on. "A below-average high school student in a small community in the west took college entrance tests along with his entire senior class. The school authorities sent his test, along with all the others, to a testing service to be machine-graded. Now the grading machine was very busy at this time of year; it ran all night as well as all day. And one night—it so happened at the precise moment that the dullard westerner's test was being perused by the machine—a mouse got into the machine's brain, shorted a circuit, or perhaps two, and caused the school lad to receive, much undeservedly, a near-perfect score. When the result of the boy's test was returned to the principal and the guidance counselor, it never occurred to them to question the machine. They blamed themselves for not having recognized this genius in disguise, this uncut and unpolished gem. So in order to atone for their sins, and since our young antihero was also a football player of some accomplishment, the principal and the guidance counselor managed to get him accepted into an eastern Ivy-League college. When he did badly in his first semester, the college advisers blamed his poor productivity on the difficult adjustment of moving from rural Montana to, let us say, suburban New Jersey, as well as on the fact of the time-consuming character of playing football. So they assigned him tutors and told him, 'Everything is really OK; you will be getting A's in no time at all.' And to make a long story short, he did. He graduated—this student of quite mediocre intelligence, this one whose life and destiny was based on a fiction—he *really* graduated with honors!" The philosopher's wife had concluded what turned out to be a rather long story. But then she added, as a sort of epilogue or moral, "Isn't that eerie—and all the more so because it is true?"

At this point the quiet wife of the instructional technologist asked with the deftness of an expert with a one-molecule-wide rapier, "How did they know it was a mouse?" There was an awkward pause, a sputter-chuckle, after which the sociologist with great finesse said: "By word of mouse!" A play with words, a pun, a ploy: it produced laughter, much laughter, loud laughter; and it demonstrated the joy of life's frictions. It had all happened so fast, too fast for squares and for square knots to be of much help. What was needed and what had been supplied was more like the ability to tie a granny with gusto! *Homo ludens:* Man the player! That is what this book is about. This book's hobby horse rocks on the revolution in the world of ideas that took place between the formal word from Huizinga in 1934 and the informal "word of mouse" deep in a Pennsylvania December.

A Modern Mythology?   In the brief span of years after Huizinga, academic disciplines that formerly seemed to have little in common suddenly found themselves doing the same sort of thing: they were structuring their subject matters around a notion of games or play. Game-theory and play-theory sprang up in sociology, philosophy, psychology, mathematics, literature, art, anthropology, communications, and even religion. And the list does not stop there. One might even be led to suspect that a universal metaphor of the theoretical disciplines was emerging. A *lingua ludica:* an emergent mythology of post-Puritan, post-Christian, postmodern man being spawned in the *nova ecclesia,* the modern university. In these latter days, it would seem, the game scholars play (including the psychologists who write about the games others play) is the game-theory game. The professoriat is construing all human meaning on the models of games and play. And judging by the way these constructions catch fire with the young generation (the first article in the under-thirty creed is: "All life is a game"), one wonders if the compellingness of this modern myth's meaning may not have more than academic significance. Especially, one wonders what religious significance there may be in this modern myth or meaning-system.

The Anatomy of the Present Work   In order to meditate on this wonder it may be useful to perform some specific exercises. The specific instances of game-theory and play-theory will be reviewed so that one may check the suspicion about the pervasiveness and persistence of game- and play-ideas in our time (Chaps. 1 and 2). A skeleton of the origin and history of the recent idea-revolution will be traced (Chap. 3). Also, the anatomy of the personal experience of games and play in the human psyche will be noted (Chap. 4). Then some interpretation will be necessary: an interpretation of play-mythology in general (Chap. 5), and a specific application of the significance of play to ideas about traditional religious meaning (Chap. 6).

But this is not all we shall attempt. Since it may well be that the notion of play is a part of a functional mythology or meaning-system and since mythologies of old are the essence of religion, this book's wonderings become finalized in an attempt at a theology of play: not only a theology *about* play (that would only be a beginning), but also a theology *made up of* play and playfulness. That is why in the Epilogue the theological argument of Chapter 6 is turned on itself and at the end a new quest is begun. It is a quest, not for a serious theology about play, but rather for a playful theology about seriousness—in fact, about Ultimate Seriousness, which is Joy.

On Cheating the Reader, or The Hobby Horse Runs Away   If this book becomes a bit playful at the end, it will be because the hobby horse (about "play" as a new mythology) is being as well fed and as passionately cared for as Earnest Calkins'. Or to put it another way, if this book becomes a bit playful, it is because musings about play that are not amusing, a book about "so fragile and quixotic an experience" as play that is not itself playful, cheats the reader. "Play is as illusive as the wind and can no more be caught by theory than the wind can be trapped in a paper bag."[2]

But this may not be so difficult an obstacle as might be imagined by some—this theorizing about play. If the reader were persuaded by the author's theorizing, be it serious or nonserious, to see all things playfully, to see with dancing eyes a vision of play, then the reader would not be cheated at all. He might then see even serious things as play, even serious books about play as themselves a bit of play. This would be like seeing the joy of life's frictions.

By being too serious about play this book may well be cheating the reader, that is true. But the opposite is no less true. By not being serious, any book risks toying with the reader who then also feels cheated. A book on play thus runs two risks and seems to be trapped in a dilemma. On the one hand, the reader will feel cheated if the author is not serious. On the other hand, the reader will also feel cheated if a book on play is too serious.

But perhaps seriousness and nonseriousness are simply two different ways man has of playing his life, and perhaps for the playful eye of *Homo ludens* these two ways are finally not all that different. They are both play. So it would not matter so much whether a book on play were serious or not. Either way *it will itself be its own point.* For the playful eye, it will make the point about play either way. And for the other eye, it would not matter anyway. What matters is a dancing eye!

It certainly would be unfair of the author to cheat the reader! Unless it meant allowing him to see playfully. But then it would not be cheating. It would be the seriousness which is play, which in turn is also the play which is Ultimate Seriousness.

But lest the reader already think this is only a play with words and is losing the fun of it, we had better turn the page and begin seriously.

PART ONE

Play's the Thing

ONE

The Contemporary Fascination with Ideas about Games and Play

Learning, the educational process, has long been associated only with the glum. We speak of the "serious" student. Our time presents a unique opportunity for learning by means of humor—a perceptive or incisive joke can be more meaningful than platitudes lying between two covers.

MARSHALL MCLUHAN

The Game Point   A curious sort of talk about play and games has become practically platitudinous in our time. It is different from the normal speaking about child's play and about football, solitaire, and monopoly games. It is different, too, from ordinary talk about such television programs as "The Dating Game," "The Mating Game," and "The Newlywed Game," though this phenomenon of making television games out of serious human meaning is interesting in itself. The curious talk about games and play worth special attention is the talk which refers to quite serious activities *as if* they were games or play. This is a curiosity. And it is especially characteristic of our age. It has become commonplace. A few examples will make the point.

"One must uphold fair play in all such serious situations," says the diplomat being politic at a news conference.

"Play the field. You must always play the field, my darling boy!" advises the mother to her son who is about to embark on a high school career of heavy dating.

"Now we must do this according to Hoyle," explains a suburban housewife to her daughter while writing out the cocktail-party invitation list.

"Com'on, you're just toying with me," teases a mistress to her lover.

"Have you noticed how much he plays around?" gossips a neighbor about the husband of a third neighbor's wife.

"You don't even cheat fair!" or "Com'on, be a sport!" says one twelve-year-old to another who gets to pick the television program.

"We've got to have more team spirit," the sales manager harangues his employees.

"I wish they'd play ball with us," says a junior executive.

"Our quarterbacks," the news media have called the last three presidents of the United States.

"Life is just a game," mumbles the eternally sophomoric college student who heard the platitude from a freshman English instructor.

Of course there are many other instances of this sort of talk in our vernacular. But it is not necessary to belabor the point.

Furthermore, popular parlance is by no means the only context in which ideas about games and play have appeared in modern life. Titles of books, movies, plays, television programs, and so on, have been flooded with "play" images. Here are just a few examples:

The War Game—a book
Games People Play—a well-known best-seller

Games—a movie

The Only Game in Town—another movie

The Name of the Game—a movie and television series

Rules of the Game—a drama

Endgame—another drama

Games Christians Play—a book

Business as a Game—a book quite unlike the one just above

The Mayor's Game—a book about a Boston mayor

The Ghetto Game—a book about social revolution

The Traitor's Game—a novel about political revolutionaries

Games of Chance—another novel

The Sex Game—a book on the sociology of interpersonal relations

The Ecological Theatre and Evolutionary Play—a zoology book

A *Play-Pray Book*—a theological book written by a nun

The Winners ⎫ the principal
Hopscotch ⎬ writings of a
End of the Game ⎭ major novelist

The Favorite Game—another book on sex

The Money Game—a best-seller

The God Game—a novel written by a seminary president

Man at Play—a book written by a famous Jesuit scholar

The Master Game—a book written by a would-be theologian

Man, Play and Games—a book by a French sociologist

Gamesmanship—a witty book of social commentary by an English literary critic

Magister Ludi (subtitled "The Bead Game")—a Nobel Prize-winning novel

And one should not omit mention of W. H. Auden's essay on folktales which is entitled "The Wish Game" and Edward Albee's first-act title "Fun and Games" and the popular song "The Game Is Over" and the advertisement for men's trousers which reads "The

Game Is Broomsticks" and the name of a professional academic journal called *Interplay* and so on and on and on.

The point of all this (i.e., the game point) is quite simple: the terms "game" and "play" are being used to describe serious non-play and real-life, nongame events and situations. Indeed, life itself is more and more being thought of as a game. It would seem that "game" and "play" are important *metaphors* of meaning in contemporary consciousness. They are important because they shift our entire way of perceiving the world and ourselves.

A metaphor—we were taught in school—is a word used to describe something it doesn't really refer to. So when Shakespeare refers to a woman by using the words "thou that art now the world's fresh ornament / and only herald to the gaudy spring," and when the sophomore of any age refers to life by using the words "game" and "play," they are both treating the terms as metaphors. A flower is not a woman; nor is life a game. At least not literally. But we see a woman quite in a new way if we think and feel about her *as if* she were a flower, "the world's fresh ornament." Similarly, we live an entirely different relationship to life—to nature, to society, and to our own selves—if we think and feel seriously about life *as if* it were the nonserious *play*ground of our being. The metaphors we use are significant; they are important for our sense of meaning. And if indeed the "game" and "play" metaphors are emerging as persistent figures of our modern thought and speech, then we may well be witnessing the molding of a new shape for all life.

The College Playground, or It's Recess All the Time in the University   The game point (i.e., that the terms "game" and "play" are being used metaphorically to describe serious nonplay and real-life, nongame events and situations) has made an impact, not only on everyday thinking and speaking and on book-titling, but especially on theory-making in traditional academic disciplines.

As was indicated in the Introduction, game-theories have emerged in mathematics, anthropology, sociology, psychology, communication and media studies, literary criticism, philosophy, and theology. It would seem that the one common element in otherwise fragmented subject matters of contemporary humanistic multiversities is the preoccupation with and use of theoretical metaphors of "game" and "play." In fact, the increasing use by original thinkers of the "game" metaphor in complicated theories is so noteworthy as to make one wonder whether the academic arts and sciences have picked up some jargon from the uncomplicated speech of the common man or whether the common man has in his everyday language picked up game-theory metaphors from complicated academic gobbledygook. Whichever is the case (and this chicken-egg circle, like so many others, may whirl both ways at once), the game point still stands.

It is as if the university, which is traditionally acknowledged to be the place where serious ideas are played with so that new knowledge and understanding may arise, has now suddenly developed into the playground where ideas about games and play are taken seriously. Or, put a bit differently, it would seem from an initial glance at the terminology used in scholarly books and articles that academicians today are not playing seriously (which would amount to *being* serious), but are simply seriously playing (which probably amounts to treating their theories simply as hypotheses, which they in fact are, instead of real reality, which of course they are not). Or perhaps the situation is even more radical: perhaps modern scholars are not even seriously playing (which may seem a contradiction in terms), but are simply, unequivocally, and without qualification . . . *playing*. Dr. James Billington, a professor of history at Princeton University, not long ago wrote in *Life* magazine a defense of humanistic higher education, at the end of which he said: "My only message is that humanities scholarship is fun."

Is this what we pay good money for when we send Johnny to college?—to learn that life is a game, including college life itself. What do Johnny's instructors mean by their game-theory metaphors? What can they possibly hope to accomplish by such talk?

What's the Name of the Game?   Precisely *that* is the name of the game today, in life and in academic scholarship. The name of the game is "asking the name of the game." Man's quest for meaning and the scholar's quest for knowledge is frequently carried on in the terminology of the "game" metaphor. The game man is playing today is *the game-game.* And to discover the game-game's rules, the boundaries of its playground, the scoring system, etc., scholars of otherwise disparate disciplines have joined together in their terminology and have, as it were, gone along with the "game."

It is not that academic disciplines ever resisted going along with the game. In fact, universities everywhere and in all times have been "playing at questions" in keeping with an original model developed by Socrates. Our contemporary Socrateses have simply played the questions out until their own questions started reflecting on the very enterprise of playing at questions. This all comes from asking the basic human-meaning question in the form of "What's the name of the game?" Here is how the reflexivity of this question works.

First, probably out of a simple and basic curiosity, some scholar hits upon the bright idea of *analyzing play*—both the play of children and the play of adults in leisure time—*as if it had some serious function,* like making better patriots or less neurotics. But this well-intending and curious scholar runs into trouble as he gets further and further into his analysis. He finds that it becomes increasingly difficult to distinguish between what is really play and what is not. Thus, a second scholar has a new hunch. He reasons that if it is so difficult to distinguish play-activity from nonplay-activity, there must be some playfulness in nonplay-activity. On the basis of his reasoning, our second hypothetical scholar raises the game question to a second dimension by *analyzing serious activity as if it were but another game, another bit of play.* His head begins to spin, however, as he realizes that in its turn *the game analysis of his game analysis might be analyzed as just a third game.* And soon he is overcome by dizziness trying to conceive the game of games of games of games, etc., on to infinity. He wonders if there may be an ultimate game, a still point, at the center of the spinning circle of plays.

If our unfortunate dizzy one recovers, he may note an important discovery: once the game and play metaphors begin to take hold, they change man's way of viewing not only situations and events *outside* himself; but also they effect *his own way of viewing his viewing* of those outside things. The metaphors change him. He now has a new criterion for his insatiable quest for meaning: namely, that the style of the quest be appropriate to its metaphoric content (the game and play of life); that "the medium be the message"; that the mode and mood of his quest be itself conceived as a game and be shaped playfully. Positivism, logical rigidity, dogmatism, literalism, and other such long-faced and long-standing leanings are out, because on the *play*ground of meaning the game points are "not quite as real or permanent, terrible, important, or logical as they seem." It's not whether you win or lose, but how. Our now fully recovered hypothetical scholar may breathe to himself, "I don't *have* to win. I just have to play. And I am doing that already. What a relief!"

But we may have moved too quickly. The relief, like the scholar, may only be hypothetical. We would do well to back up and demonstrate the hypotheses of the last two paragraphs by examining some actual cases of the game-theorizing of recent scholars. In this way we may not only demonstrate the reflexive implication of game-theory but also articulate *directly* the game point of academia referred to earlier. The specific cases reviewed in the next chapter will not exhaust the numerous possible examples that might be examined. These have been chosen because they are typical of their field and because they demonstrate the movement of the three basic forms of academic use of "game" and "play" images: (1) the analysis of play activity as if it had a serious function; (2) the analysis of serious activity as if it had a play function; and (3) the analysis of analyses of serious and play activity as if they were a game . . . the game-game.

TWO

The Contemporary Academic Game of Games

All this, when will all this have been . . . just play?
SAMUEL BECKETT

Anthropology and Ethnology   Sooner or later most academic studies of games and play refer back to the central work of the Dutch historian of culture, JOHAN HUIZINGA. We have already noted how this scholar took for the topic of a 1933 lecture the title, "The Cultural Limits of Play and the Serious." The idea for this lecture and for the book which followed it (*Homo Ludens*, 1938) came to Huizinga while at work on a study of the cultural history of the Middle Ages.[1] He was trying to understand why medieval Christendom artificially maintained such cultural elements of a long-forgotten past as codes of honor, heraldry, chivalric orders and tournaments, courtly demeanor, etc. It occurred to him that these elements of medieval society were the vestiges of primeval initiation rites which had their origin in sacred play and were being carried on in the spirit of play in the Middle Ages. Though play, they had a serious function for society: they produced a culture. Play, Huizinga hypothesized, may be viewed as the basis of culture.

In *Homo Ludens* ("Man the Player") Huizinga attempts to demonstrate his hypothesis that play is indeed the basis of culture. On the basis of the serious analyses of play which preceded his own work, he defines play-activity as a voluntary activity, absorbing to the player yet existing outside the scope of everyday life, proceeding within fixed limits and according to fixed rules, promoting socialization in small groups, which have secret regulations and yielding no material gain. Huizinga then proceeds to trace the concept of play through its variations of meaning in such diverse language groups as Chinese, Blackfoot, Sanskrit, Latin, Greek, German, etc. He discovers not only that some languages (e.g., Sanskrit) have several words for play; not only that there is an interesting relation between the verb for "play" and its object (e.g., in German you "play play"—*spielen ein Spiel*—whereas in English you "play a game," the noun and verb being a doublet and being therefore conceived as separable entities); not only that play and love-making are closely linked (e.g., the Sanskrit term *krīdaratnam*, which means "copulation," is literally translated "the jewel of games"); but also, and most importantly, that "play" is not to be conceived as the opposite of "serious" or "earnest" (e.g., see the Hebrew in 2 Samuel 2:14 where "play" means "kill the enemy," or see Shakespeare's *Tempest*, line 9 of the first scene, where "play at the oars" means "work hard at rowing").

Huizinga concludes that

the two terms [i.e., "play" and "earnest"] are not of equal value: play is positive, earnest negative. The significance of "earnest" is defined by and exhausted in the negation of "play"—earnest is simply "not playing" and nothing more. The significance of "play," on the other hand, is by no means defined or exhausted by calling it "not-earnest," or "not serious." Play is a thing by itself. The play-concept as such is of a higher order than is seriousness. For seriousness seeks to exclude play, whereas play can very well include seriousness.[2]

Having established a definition of play and having surveyed its manifold connotations, the author notes that the initial culture formation of great civilizations, like the Greek one, is often to be found in play-contests (agōns) which manifest themselves in sacred rituals, heroic feats, sports, etc. As these societies pass out of an early agonistic and heroic phase, civilization becomes complex and "is gradually smothered under a rank layer of ideas, systems of thought and knowledge, doctrines, rules and regulations, moralities and conventions which have all lost touch with play." Or so it would seem. But Huizinga shows in the remainder of his book that such apparently nonplay—cultural activities as law, war, education, poetry, myth-making, philosophy, and art—have their bases in play whether the players, who often pretend to be workers, admit to it or not.

Huizinga's argument is fascinating and compelling. It compels one to view culture *sub specie ludi*, from the point of view of play. And this does not mean "not seriously." Play, as Huizinga has carefully shown, is a category lying beyond the dichotomy of serious/not-serious. If we have been so long trapped into thinking seriously about life and meaning in categories of seriousness, Huizinga enables us to transcend such a bind by arguing the priority of play to seriousness and by showing that it is possible to see "play" as a term lying outside the serious/not-serious options. We have a new option. We may view all culture *sub specie ludi*.

Huizinga has used the term play *as a metaphor to explain serious cultural meaning;* or in the terms of Chapter 1, he analyzed serious activity as if it had a play function. By showing us this fascinating possibility, he also opens the possibility of the use of play as the basic category, not only for studies of culture, but also for all human studies. This is why most scholars developing theories about games and play sooner or later refer back to the work of Johan Huizinga.

JOSEPH CAMPBELL is one such scholar. In introducing his four-volume study of man's myths (*The Masks of God*, vol. 1, *Primitive Mythology*, 1959) Campbell defines the function of myth—the key term of his study of human cultures—by referring to a line from *Homo Ludens:* "In all the wild imaginings of mythology a fanciful spirit is playing on the border-line between jest and earnest." Campbell elaborates the point in keeping with Huizinga's thesis, applying that thesis to the specific area-study of comparative mythology.

Campbell's researches have led him to view myth as the basis of a people's meaning. But the basis for the meaning-function of myth, Campbell argues, is play. The "logic" of myth, like the "logic" of play, is the "logic" of "as if." The realm of a man's myth is described as "the world of the gods and demons, the carnival of their masks and the curious game of 'as if' in which the festival of the lived myth abrogates all the laws of time, letting the dead swim back to life, and the 'once upon a time' become the very present."[3] Campbell suggests that "such a highly played game of 'as if' frees our mind and spirit, on the one hand, from the presumption of theology, which pretends to know the laws of God, and, on the other, from the bondage of reason, whose laws do not apply beyond the horizon of human experience."[4] Campbell, like Huizinga, is performing a serious analysis of society's seriousness as if it were at base a bit of play.

But not all scholars who are students of society and who draw upon the metaphor of "play" in their studies are as ready to agree with Huizinga as is Campbell. ADOLF JENSEN and ROGER CALLOIS, both European social anthropologists, utilize Huizinga's work as their starting point, but both are eager to modify his views in keeping with their own findings. It may be observed that their work, however, is not a contradiction of Huizinga's thesis, because they are not in fact doing the same thing he is doing. They are not performing an analysis of culture's seriousness as if it were play (where play is a *metaphor* of social meaning). They are, rather, performing an analysis of culture's actual play as if it had a serious function. Therefore, while Jensen and Callois may modify some of the details of Huizinga's work, they in no way negate it. For them "play" is intended quite literally, while for Huizinga "play" is used as a metaphor.

Huizinga had referred to the work of Adolf Jensen in *Homo Ludens*. He had utilized Jensen's research on the attitudes of primitive peoples toward their religious festivals. Jensen had reported that primitive men know quite well that the ghosts and witch-doctor's masks are "not real." But the participants in primitive rites are seized by the awe of the ritual anyway. Huizinga quotes Jensen as saying that "their position is much like that of parents playing Santa Claus for their children: they know of the mask, but hide it from them." These data from Jensen's ethnological researches are one more argument, or so Huizinga construes it, for a play basis of culture.

Jensen himself responds to Huizinga's argument in a book published in 1951, entitled, *Mythos und Kult bei Naturvölken* (English translation: *Myth and Cult among Primitive Peoples*, 1963). Jensen is grateful to Huizinga for what the former calls the elucidation of "the play aspect of cult" and he says, "I believe that ethnology can accept Huizinga's ideas without the slightest hesitation." Yet where play is a metaphor of the basis of all culture for Huizinga, for Jensen it is but one aspect of cult, which is itself but one aspect of culture. In fact it turns out that Jensen himself has more than a "slightest hesitation" about Huizinga's argument.

Jensen notes that while all cultic activities of primitive peoples seem to have a dimension of play inherent in them, by no means does all human play have a cultic dimension to it. Therefore he wonders if it is not important to distinguish more clearly than Huizinga does between the games of children, which he characterizes as "mere play," and the play of cult, which includes an "additional mental element" of a sacred character. By reinstating the distinction between sacred and secular forms of play, Jensen is better able to analyze various types of human social behavior, but he does this at the cost of implying a distinction between serious play (sacred cult) and nonserious play (children's games), a distinction which the category of play had transcended and reunified in the work of Huizinga. The point of the dispute is simply that Jensen is more concerned to analyze accurately the serious (i.e., cultic and sacred) aspects of man's play. Huizinga, on the other hand is concerned to analyze the playful aspects of man's serious activity, a task whose purpose is best fulfilled when the dichotomies of sacred and secular, serious and nonserious, etc., are transcended in a unified scheme of human meaning.

Roger Callois, like Jensen, speaks initially in praise of Huizinga's work. As editor of the journal *Diogenes* he writes: "*Homo Ludens* is the most important work in the philosophy of history in our century." But also like Jensen, his praise soon turns to critique. Writing in *Les Jeux et les hommes*, 1958 (English translation: *Man, Play and Games*, 1961), Callois challenges Huizinga's definition of play. Callois finds the definition too broad in its inclusion of the elements of secrecy and mystery. He finds in his own researches that playing and being playful about human activity tend to remove the secrecy and mystery that might be involved in that activity. He also feels that when the secret or mysterious activity is sacramental the activity can no longer be called "play." Furthermore, Callois thinks Huizinga's definition is too narrow in excluding from the play-sphere human activity which results in material gain. Callois himself is eager to discover a theory of games and play which will include such activity as gambling, racing, lotteries, casinos, etc.

The theory of games and play that Callois develops speaks especially to this latter "deficiency" in Huizinga's definition. Callois categorizes the games men and children play under two sets of rubrics. The first is a charting of various types of games: *agon,* or competition; *alea,* or chance; *mimicry,* or simulation; and *ilinx,* or vertigo. The second set of classifications is a scale, not of types of games, but of ways of playing: it moves from *paidia,* which is characterized by improvisation and freedom, to *ludus,* which is characterized by rules and orderly regulation. The diagram below indicates how these two sets of rubrics work to classify all the games men and children play.

Callois's classification of games is essentially a work which might be called a sociology of the games men and children play. Yet he intends his analysis to have a broader function. He says: "I have not only undertaken a sociology of games, I have the idea of laying the foundations for a sociology *derived from games.*" To the end

Classification of Games[5]

	AGON (*Competition*)	ALEA (*Chance*)	MIMICRY (*Simulation*)	ILINX (*Vertigo*)
PAIDIA				
Tumult	Racing	Counting-out	Child's	Whirling
Agitation	Wrestling	rhymes	imitation	Riding
Immoderate	Athletics	Heads or tails	Games of	Swinging
laughter	Boxing		illusion	Waltzing
Kite flying	Chess	Betting	Tag	
Solitaire	Billiards	Roulette	Disguises	Volador
Patience	Football			Carnivals
Crossword	Sports	Simple, complex,		Skiing
puzzles	in general	and continuing	Theater	Mountain
		lotteries	Spectacles	climbing
			in general	Tightrope
LUDUS				walking

N.B. In each vertical column games are classified in such an order that the *paidia* element is constantly decreasing while the *ludus* element is ever increasing.

of this broader purpose, the purpose not only of seriously analyzing games but also of making games the basis for a serious sociology, Callois writes a chapter on "The Social Function of Games" and another on "The Corruption of Games." He indicates how, as games become more and more regulated (i.e., as they move toward *ludus* away from *paidia*), they tend to be performed in groups and before crowds. This is obvious, of course. But Callois has more than this in mind when he speaks of the "social function of games." He notes that each type of game (i.e., *agon, alea, mimicry,* and *ilinx*) seems to produce a corresponding nongame activity in serious everyday life. And furthermore, he shows how each type of game activity, if pursued in excess and without balance and harmony, tends to some social corruption. The chart on page 25 may make this aspect of Callois's argument easier to grasp.

By this sort of analysis Callois hopes to carry on Huizinga's thesis that "the spirit of play is essential to culture." But he hopes to complement Huizinga's work by filling in a prior step to the argument of that work: namely, an analysis of games which shows them to be "historically the residues of culture." Callois is certainly correct in noting that if Huizinga is to make "play" and "games" the base metaphor for all culture, the content of this metaphor must first be expanded and elucidated. Yet in attempting to provide the necessary first step in an analysis that makes play a "residue of culture," Callois is trying the impossible. He wants to affirm Huizinga's judgment that play is the basis of culture and at the same time affirm the contrary judgment that play is the result of culture. He wants to have it both ways, as he shows in statements like this one:

In the end, the question of knowing which preceded the other, play or the serious, is a vain one. To explain games as derived from laws, customs, and liturgies, or in reverse to explain jurisprudence, liturgy, and the rules for strategy, syllogisms, or esthetics as a derivation of

The Social Function of Games[6]

	Cultural Forms Found at the Margins of the Social Order	Institutional Forms Integrated into Social Life	Corruption
AGON (*Competition*)	Sports	Economic competition Competitive examinations	Violence Will to Power Trickery
ALEA (*Chance*)	Lotteries Casinos Hippodromes Pari-mutuels	Speculation on the stock market	Superstition Astrology, etc.
MIMICRY (*Simulation*)	Carnival Theater Cinema Hero-worship	Uniforms Ceremonial etiquette	Alienation Split personality
ILINX (*Vertigo*)	Mountain climbing Skiing Tightrope walking Speed	Professions requiring control of vertigo [airline pilot, etc.]	Alcoholism and drugs

play, are complementary, equally fruitful operations provided they are not regarded as mutually exclusive. The structures of play and reality are often identical, but the respective activities that they subsume are not reducible to each other in time or place. They always take place in domains that are incompatible.[7]

To argue that play and serious social intercourse "take place in domains that are incompatible," and to argue that "the structures of play and reality are often identical," is to treat "games" and "play" literally. *Callois has succeeded in speaking seriously about games and play.* In fact, his analysis is certainly one of the more ingenious that has been devised. But his work should not be confused with the enterprise of speaking about seriousness as if it were play, as for example Huizinga was doing. The two enterprises—Callois is right in this—are complementary. But because of his literal use of the terms "games" and "play," Callois will have to be satisfied in having produced a "sociology of games." He will have to leave to others the broader task of producing a "sociology derived from games."

Sociology and Economics   The task of deriving a sociology from the "game" metaphor, parallel to the task of deriving a cultural anthropology from the "play" metaphor, was begun long before Callois was attempting to lay the foundations for it. In fact, it was begun a year after Huizinga's famous lecture and four years prior to the publication of his *Homo Ludens*. The roots of game-theory in sociology are to be found in a brief section of *Mind, Self, and Society* (1934), written by a University of Chicago social philosopher, GEORGE HERBERT MEAD. Mead utilized an analysis of the games and play of children to show the conditions "under which the self arises as an object." He argued that in games and play, as in mastery of language, children discover an identity as individuals over against the collectivity of the social order.[8] It is this sort of argument that makes Mead the father of play-theory in sociology.[9] Play-theory in this field is generally termed "role-theory," and along with "the sociology of knowledge," whose sires were Max Scheler and Karl Mannheim, it accounts for most of the work being done in contemporary sociology.

Harvard professor TALCOTT PARSONS has integrated the "playing-a-role" theories of the self which have emerged in anthropology, sociology, and psychology. But it remained for a sociologist by the name of ERVING GOFFMAN to articulate a sociological role-theory that would pick up from George Herbert Mead the metaphor of "play" and allow it to have its full game-function as well as its dramatic and theatrical overtones. He first achieved such an articulation in a book titled *The Presentation of Self in Everyday Life* (1959). The theories presented in it have been supplemented and amplified in more recent works such as *Interaction Ritual: Essays on Face-to-Face Behavior* (1967), and *Encounters: Two Studies in the Sociology of Interaction* (1961).

Goffman is primarily concerned to create a theory for understanding the structure and dynamics of "face-to-face" interaction between persons in social situations. He develops such a theory around the basic terms "performance," "role," "teams," "part," "routine"—the last term being borrowed from John von Neumann and Oskar Morgenstern's mathematical game-theory, and the first, from the work of men like George Herbert Mead. By utilizing these terms Goffman is able to suggest that the structure of the self may best be understood when it is seen in the context of a performance of role that is presented to other selves, i.e., to a team or audience. Understood in this social context the self is seen to be composed of two parts: a "performer" that fabricates roles and stages a performance, and a "character" which is usually "a fine one, whose spirit, strength, and other sterling qualities the performance was designed to evoke." Men go through life, Goffman supposes, "training for a part." Sometimes the training pays off and the performance is "well oiled" and impressions "flow from it fast enough to put us in the grips of one of our types of reality," but on other occasions, since "the whole machinery of self-production is cumbersome," the performance "breaks down, exposing its separate components: back region control; team collusion; audience tact; and so forth."[10]

In all this it is clear how Goffman exploits the theatrical and dramatic implications of the term "play" in his sociology. How he broadens the "play" metaphor to include "game" connotations becomes clearer in two later essays, "Fun and Games" (*Encounters*, 1961) and "Where the Action Is" (*Interaction Ritual*, 1967).

In the latter essay Goffman inquires into the logic underlying the action of society by analyzing the significance of a recent English idiom, "where the action is," and abstracting it to the status of a principle of the social order. He begins with an epigram and an anecdote. The epigram is a saying attributed to the world-famous tightrope artist Karl Wallenda, spoken on the occasion of his going back up to the high wire after his troupe's fatal Detroit accident some years ago. He is supposed to have said: "To be on the high wire is life; the rest is waiting." Goffman follows this epigram with an anecdote which he intends to be a paradigm example of all "action" activity.

Two boys together find a nickel in their path and decide that one will toss and the other call to see who keeps it. They agree, then, to engage in a *play*, or, as probabilists call it, a *gamble*—in this case one go at the *game* of coin-tossing. . . .

What a player has in hand and undergoes a chance of losing is his stake or *bet*. What the play gives him a chance of winning that he doesn't already have can be called his *prize*. The *payoff* for him is the prize that he wins or the bet that he loses. Bet and prize together may be called the *pot*. . . .

In the degree to which a play is a means of acquiring a prize, it is an *opportunity;* in the degree to which it is a threat to one's bet, it is a *risk*. . . .

Each of our coin tossers can be defined as having a life course in which the finding of a nickel has not been anticipated. Without the find, life would go forward as expected. Each boy can then conceive of his situation as affording him a gain or returning him to what is only normal. A chance-taking of this kind can be called opportunity without risk. Were a bully to approach one of the boys and toss him for a nickel taken from the boy's own pocket (and this happens in city neighborhoods), we could then speak of a risk without opportunity. In daily life, risks and opportunities usually occur together, and in all combinations. . . .

A crucial feature of coin-tossing is its temporal phases. The boys must decide to settle the matter by tossing; they must align themselves physically; they must decide how much of the nickel will be gambled on the toss and who will take which outcome; through stance and gesture they must commit themselves to the gamble and thereby pass the point of no return. This is the bet-making or *squaring off phase.* Next there is the in-play or *determination phase,* during which relevant causal forces actively and determinatively produce the outcome. Then comes the revelatory or *disclosive* phase, the time between determination and informing of the participants. This period is likely to be very brief, to differ among sets of participants differently placed relative to the decision machinery, and to possess a special suspensefulness of its own. Finally there is the *settlement phase,* beginning when the outcome has been disclosed and lasting until losses have been paid up and gains collected. . . .

Given these distinctions in the phases of play, it is easy to attend to a feature of simple games of chance that might otherwise be taken for granted. Once a play is undertaken, its determination, disclosure, and settlement usually follow quickly, often before another bet is made. . . . Everyday life is usually quite different. Certainly the individual makes bets and takes chances in regard to daily living, as when, for example, he decides to take one job instead of another or to move from one state to another. Further, at certain junctures he may have to make numerous vital decisions at the same time and hence briefly maintain a very high rate of bet-making. But ordinarily the determination phase—the period during which the consequences of his bet are determined—will be long, sometimes extending over decades, followed by disclosure and settlement phases that are themselves lengthy. The distinctive property of games and contests is that once the bet has been made, *outcome is determined and payoff awarded all in the same breath of experience.* A single sharp focus of awareness is sustained at high pitch during the full span of the play.[11]

Goffman derives the following principles from this anecdotal analysis: "Action is to be found wherever the individual knowingly takes consequential chances perceived as avoidable,"[12] with the further modification that "when persons go to where the action is, they often go to a place where there is an increase, not in the chances taken, but in the chances that they will be obliged to take chances."[13] It is clear that Goffman has derived a principle of society's activity that is based upon the model of a game. He has utilized the game metaphor as a basis for understanding society's serious activity.

PETER BERGER, a sociologist at the New School for Social Research in New York City, has done much the same thing in *The Precarious Vision: A Sociologist Looks at Social Fictions and Christian Faith* (1961). He mentions his gratitude for Goffman's work in a footnote but is himself more concerned to develop a picture of social "reality" which will take a middle ground between role-theory in sociology (i.e., play and game theory) and sociology of knowledge. Nonetheless, Berger adopts the terminology of "social game" from GEORGE SIMMEL and he utilizes the whole complex of base terms "play," "role," etc., from game theoreticians.

Berger pictures social "reality" as having a precarious status. The society we assume to be "reality" turns out, according to Berger's precarious vision, to be a set of "social fictions" (Mead's "roles" and Goffman's "performances"). These "fictions" determine human actions, but, because they are "fictions," also become the basis for freedom if they can be broken through with a well-aimed ploy. The playful ploy properly administered pricks the balloon of the phoniness of society's artificial structure and opens the possibility of free and morally responsible human activity. When man sees the gaminess of society he is then able not to take its bourgeois demands so seriously and may therefore break out of the requirements of the gray-flannel prison suit and the split-level trap.

By this sort of theorizing Berger's sociology, like Goffman's, becomes an example *par excellence* of the use of the "game" and "play" metaphors in a serious analysis of society's seriousness. Not only does Berger imply a critique of societal patterns of behavior by referring to their "gamey" characteristics, but he also views society as learning to "play the game" of socialization, a process without which men would be atoms in an atomized world rather than members of cohesive groups. Seeing the character of society as like that of a game enables the analyst of society's meaning and function to understand the process by which men are able to bind themselves together in the teamwork which we know as community.[14]

The broad possibilities of viewing society as having the character of a game are seen in two examples of the expansion of the use of the "game" metaphor in studies of society beyond those of cultural history (Huizinga, Campbell, Callois, Jensen) and of sociology (Mead, Simmel, Goffman, Berger). The examples we have in mind are the fields of ecology and economics.

NIGEL CALDER, an English ecologist, published a book in 1967 which argues forcefully for a plan to economize society's natural resources. The book's intriguing title is *Eden Was No Garden,* and the argument suggests that man should conceive of himself as a "game-keeper." The term has a double meaning. Not only should man keep watch over game, i.e., over his natural environment. Man should also conserve the "environment game," i.e., society itself.

Calder describes the problem-situation which faces contemporary man:

By about the end of this century there will be an embarrassment of material riches in many countries. The computer-communications network will be substantially complete. By then, too, large-scale synthetic food production will have begun and, given sufficient effort, should be reaching the point at which agricultural production no longer needs to grow to keep abreast of population; the subsequent decline of agriculture will, however, be relatively slow, so that it may not be until well into the twenty-first century that the large tracts of farmland have been released for restoration of the wilderness.[15]

In the face of this situation we need, Calder feels, to

reconstruct our ideas to cope with the new "leisured" existence and to eradicate the idea of the importance of work which has dogged us since the invention of agriculture. . . . To suggest that nothing short of a major reconstruction of our way of life is needed to defeat the boredom of leisured affluence may seem pessimistic to conservative minds; and to go on to propose that we have to treat life as a huge game may strike as absurd or monstrous the more radically-minded people who tend in a puritanical sense to be conservative. But I use the word "game" advisedly. By a quirk of derivation, the English use that term both for a recreation and for hunted animals. If we stick firmly to the notion that man is by evolutionary design a hunter, we may be able to discover how we should live. It is no pun or idle metaphor to see social institutions such as have existed since the dawn of agriculture as an elaborate game, the prizes of which are individual wealth and power.[16]

Calder goes on to analyze some of the games of society that man has played through the years: e.g., the paleolithic game; the neolithic/present-day game; gambling games; simulated-skills games; miscellaneous tasks games; sports games; the sex game;[17] ritual games; entertainment games; the knowledge game; the "big-science" game; the beautification game; the conservation game. Calder calls for a combination of the last four of these into a radically new game, "an environment game," whose "overall purpose is to enhance, by the efforts of the individual and his community, the individual's own knowledge and enjoyment of the terrestrial environment, natural and human. The aim would be to manipulate non-monetary wealth and human knowledge in order to maximize them, for these are themselves the rewards of the game. It is a non-zero-sum game [i.e., a game in which what one man wins another man need not necessarily lose]." [18] It is this environment game that Calder has in mind when he suggests that man today should think of himself as a "game-keeper." The results, he hopes, would be a "cheerful wilderness." For "Eden was no garden" filled with work and agricultural production; it was, rather, a wild and wonderful paleolithic plain of a great hunt culture.

The pseudonymous "ADAM SMITH" has a bit different vision of our contemporary wilderness, a wilderness of high finance and big business. Yet his use of the "game" metaphor to analyze the economic aspect of society is as fascinating as Calder's use of it in ecology. In fact it is so fascinating that it earned *The Money Game* (1968) a number-one spot on the best-seller list only a few weeks after publication.

The Money Game gets its title and its beginning from a somewhat surprising saying of a British economist, JOHN MAYNARD KEYNES (1883–1946): "The game of professional investment is intolerably boring and overexacting to anyone who is entirely exempt from the gambling instinct; whilst he who has it must pay to this propensity the appropriate toll."

"Adam Smith" notes the work in game-theory of mathematicians von Neumann and Morgenstern, and then comments on the Keynes citation:

> . . . game theory has had a tremendous impact on our national life; it influences how our defense decisions are made and how the marketing strategies of great corporations are worked out. What is game theory? You could say it is an attempt to quantify and work through the actions of players in a game, to measure their options continuously. Or, to be more formal, game theory is a branch of mathematics that aims to analyze problems of conflict by abstracting common strategic

features for study in theoretical models. (You can tell by the phrasing of that last sentence that I have the book [by von Neumann and Morgenstern] before me, so let us go on.) By stressing strategic aspects, i.e., those controlled by the participants, it goes beyond the classic theory of probability, in which the treatment of games is limited to aspects of pure chance. Drs. von Neumann and Morgenstern worked through systems that incorporated conflicting interests, incomplete information, and the interplay of free rational decision and choice. They started with dual games, zero sum two-person games, i.e., those in which one player wins what the other loses. At the other end you have something like the stock market, an infinite n-person game. (N is one of the letters economists use when they don't know something.) The stock market is probably temporarily too complex even for the Game Theoreticians, but I suppose some day even it will become a serious candidate for quantification and equations. I bring this up only because I think the market is both a game and a Game, i.e., both sport, frolic, fun, and play, and a subject for continuously measurable options. If it is a game, then we can relieve ourselves of some of the heavy and possibly crippling emotions that individuals carry into investing, because in a game the winning of the stake is clearly defined. Anything else becomes irrelevant.[19]

The author then undertakes an almost three-hundred-page description of "the money game" which includes chapters such as: "The Broker as Witch-Doctor," "My Friend the Gnome of Zurich Says a Major Money Crisis Is on Its Way," "If All the Half Dollars Have Disappeared, Is Something Sinister Gaining on Us?" etc. In these and other entertaining, as well as enlightening, chapters the author indicates "the rules of the Game." He acknowledges at the end that there may be some who will be offended by the idea of the management of money as a game. "Money, they would say, is serious business, no laughing matter, and certainly nothing that should suggest sport, frolic, fun and play." The author's response is direct: "It may be that the Game element in money is the most harmless of all the elements present." The reason for this is not only that the game-viewpoint may relieve "some of the heavy and possibly crippling emotions that individuals carry into investing," as we have already noted. It is also based on the author's understanding of *purposiveness*.

"What does the purposive investor seek? 'The purposive man,'"— the author is quoting Keynes again—"'is always trying to secure a spurious and delusive immortality for his acts by pushing his interest in them forward into time. He does not love his cat, but his cat's kittens; nor, in truth, the kittens, but only the kittens' kittens, and so on forward for ever to the end of cat-dom. For him jam is not jam unless it is a case of jam tomorrow and never jam today. Thus by pushing his jam always forward into the future, he strives to secure for his act of boiling it an immortality.'" But the game-theoretician knows there is a large amount of unreality in such a man of purpose. So, our pseudonymous author concludes:

> You know, in the end, that so deep-seated an impulse could not be merely the amusement that comes with a Game. The compounding of wealth, like the building of the City, is part of the much older game of life against death. The immortality is spurious because that particular wheel is fixed; you do have to lose in the end. That is the way the senior game is set up: You can't take it with you.

Thus, having revealed the dynamic that makes the money game go round, the author ends his book with a sort of parody benediction.

> Now that you know some of the things as they are and not as they ought to be, perhaps you will know whether to take the Game or leave it alone. You have to make your own choice, and there are many other and more productive outlets for time and energy. Until daylight, I wish you the joys of the Game.[20]

The conclusion is in keeping with the style throughout, which, appropriate to the content of the book, has itself been lighthearted, playful. Reading the book is a sort of game, which in the end the reader is to discover has in fact been a game of life and death. The meeting of style and content gives the book an integrity that might be missed by the casual reader because of the work's *apparent* nonseriousness.

We predicted in Chapter 1 that this might happen in game-theory: that an analysis of play activity as if it had a serious function would lead to an analysis of serious activity as if it had a play function, and that finally, both would lead the writers of these first two analyses to view the analysis of their analyses as if they themselves were a game . . . the game-game, we called it.

But not only is this the case with "Smith" and to some extent Calder. Already Erving Goffman and Peter Berger had intimations that this is the way in which the style of academic studies might go. In *The Precarious Vision,* Berger protests that his understanding of society as a game does not imply a rejection of the serious study of that society. Yet he does go as far as to admit that the introduction of the metaphors of "game" and "play" into serious studies may cause those studies themselves to take on a "comic perspective." [21] If by saying this Berger opens a door, Goffman walks right into it or perhaps through it at the end of his *Presentation of Self in Everyday Life:*

> And now a final comment. In developing the conceptual framework employed in this report, some language of the stage was used. . . . The claim that all the world's a stage is sufficiently commonplace for readers to be familiar with its limitations and tolerant of its presentation, knowing that at any time they will easily be able to demonstrate to themselves that it is not to be taken too seriously. . . . And so here the language and mask of the stage will be dropped. Scaffolds, after all, are to build other things with, and should be erected with an eye to taking them down.[22]

And apparently this author is including the theoretical scaffolding which is built up in the two hundred and fifty-three pages that precede this one. That is, game-theory, whether the author wishes and acknowledges it or not, finally impinges upon itself. When this is acknowledged by the theoretician, new possibilities open up for academic disciplines.

One example of these *new possibilities* of disciplines whose method and subject matter are appropriate to each other is contained in the works of an author cited and commended by both Berger and Goffman. The author is STEPHEN POTTER. Though he is by training an interpreter of English literature and though he has published "serious" critical works on D. H. Lawrence and Coleridge, he is best known for his "nonserious" studies of society: *One-Upmanship; The Theory and Practice of Gamesmanship; Some Notes on Lifemanship; Anti-Woo;* etc. Potter's amusing treatments of "the art of winning games without actually cheating" are considered, at least by Berger and Goffman, to contain a quite serious picture of the interaction of persons in society. And in order to be "quite serious" about something "nonserious," an "amusing treatment" is in order. Method is appropriate to subject matter. Or put differently, the subject impinges itself on the style of the writer, rather than the writer forcing his own self, about which he may be rather serious, onto the subject in question.

Psychology Just as in sociology, so in psychology there are, on the one hand, theories that attribute to the play of children a serious function, and, on the other, theories that attribute a playful function to the seriousness of adults. We shall first review four typical, but diverse, psychologies which seriously analyze play as if it had a serious function.

ÉDOUARD CLAPARÈDE, a professor of experimental psychology in Geneva, Switzerland, wrote a widely distributed textbook, *Psychologie de l'enfant et pédagogie expérimentale,* whose fourth edition was translated into English and published in 1911 under the title, *Experimental Pedagogy and the Psychology of the Child*. During the course of this study the author raised the question, "Of what use is childhood?" He found the clue to its answer in an analysis of the reasons children play. Men must be children before they are adults because they need to play. The author indicates why this is so.

Claparède reviewed the theories of play proposed by his nineteenth-century predecessors: the poet Schiller, the philosopher Spencer, the psychologist Hall, the anthropologist Groos, etc. Claparède discovered among the works of these theorists four categories of play-theory. (1) A theory of relaxation held that men and children play because their minds and bodies need rest in order that they might go on working. (2) A theory of superfluous energy held that play is the activity that enables man and child to get rid of excess energy in acceptable activity. (3) A theory of atavism proposed that play is nothing but the persistence of certain rudimentary functions which have become useless and especially are useless in adult serious activity, much like the tadpole's tail. Children must play, therefore, so they will not need to pursue certain immature activities in their mature years. (4) A theory of preparatory exercise held that play is practice for the serious work of adult life. It has a teaching function. Or, as one writer had put it, "it is not because the animal is young that he plays, but that he has youth because he needs to play."

It is this last theory that Claparède supports. He points out that children play sensory games, motor games, psychic games, wrestling games, hunting games, social games, family games—all of which tend to be games of imitation. The child is practicing how to become an adult. If children do not play enough or if they do not play properly, their development will be arrested. "Moles," the author says in a footnote, "have atrophied eyes because they have not 'played' enough with light."

A somewhat different psychological evaluation of the serious purpose of play was offered in 1927 by a team of psychologists, HARVEY C. LEHMAN and PAUL A. WITTY, who were from the School of Education of the University of Kansas. Their book, *The Psychology of Play Activities,* like Claparède's, reviews previous play-theories in psychology, omitting, interestingly enough, Claparède's work. They include however psychologies of play which were at Claparède's disposal, but which he excluded, notably, the theories of Sigmund Freud.

Lehman and Witty content themselves, as they put it, "with a discussion of the conditions under which various types of play occur." They are doubtful that play can be "explained" by rational theories, attempts which they liken to explaining what electricity "really is" as opposed to showing what it *does:* "You can make an electrician mad . . . by interrupting his explanation of a dynamo by asking: 'But you cannot tell me what electricity really is.' The electrician does not care a rap what electricity 'really is' . . . if there really is any meaning to that phrase. All he wants to know is what he can do with it." [23] The authors, therefore, are not content with academicians who attempt to *explain* "play" and who in the process are likely explaining only their own explanations.

Thus after reviewing the surplus-energy theory, the practice or preparatory theory, the pleasure-gratification theory (Freud), etc., the authors assert a working definition of play to be used in their descriptive (as opposed to explanatory) work. "Play," they say, "may be regarded as consisting largely of the activities in which the individual engages 'just because he wants to.' The above statement has certain limitations. At certain times an individual may eat, sleep, etc., 'just because he wants to.' Of course such activities would not be regarded as play. But most of the remaining activities in the behavior stream (when such purely physiological reactions as eating, sleeping, etc., are eliminated) in which the child takes part *of his own volition* may be considered his play life." [24]

This free-will/volitional theory of play may be referred to as the "Just Because I Want To" theory, or, for short, as "Play Just Because."

A third analysis of the play-function has been developed by JEAN PIAGET, a Swiss scholar who is perhaps the leading child psychologist in the world today. Piaget has written many books and articles on the serious function of the play of children, but for purposes of the present discussion one of these writings is most important, namely, *Play, Dreams and Imitation in Childhood* (published in 1951 as the English translation of *La Formation du symbole*). There are references in this book to the work of Claparède and to the work of Lehman and Witty, as well as to the works of those whom these men review; but the argument concerning play developed in Piaget's work is informed more by empirical observation of children at play in his own school, the *Maison des Petits*, in Geneva, than it is dependent upon the opinions about play developed by other speculative scholars. Indeed, Piaget's analysis of the play of children is far and away the most sophisticated and complex analysis of the serious function of play we have at our disposal. We shall examine Piaget's arguments more closely in Chapter 4. For now a simple summary must suffice.

There are three stages of child's play according to Piaget's findings. The first stage, between birth and age two, is the beginning of play. The second stage, between two and seven, is the period of the transformation of play into game. And the third stage, between eight and twelve, is the time of the decline of child's play.

There is an increase in work-activity in the third stage. This is important for proper development and for socialization. Indeed, the only games that persist at the adult stage are "socialized games, controlled by rules." "In games with rules there is a subtle equilibrium between assimilation to the ego—the principle of all play—and social life. There is still sensory-motor or intellectual satisfaction, and there is also the chance of individual victory over others, but these satisfactions are as it were made 'legitimate' by the rules of the game, through which competition is controlled by a collective discipline, with a code of honour and fair play." [25]

It is not altogether obvious to ARNOLD R. BEISSER, a practicing California psychiatrist and professor, that there is psychic "equilibrium" in the games-with-rules which adults play. In *The Madness in Sports: Psychosocial Observations on Sports* (1967), Beisser has recorded the case studies of a basketball player, a football player, a golfer, a tennis player, a boxer, and a weight-lifter, all of whom were outstanding in their particular sports and all of whom came to Beisser (at one time himself a tournament tennis player) for psychiatric treatment.

The true stories are arresting reading for those in a culture such as ours which more and more witnesses to the fascination of what Beisser calls "the American seasonal masculinity rites" on television. The conclusions reached by the author are not wholly negative. He finds four serious functions in sports: (1) "They provide an arena for the expression of many physical actions stimulated by the culture but precluded by the rules of everyday life"; (2) "They provide an opportunity for the symbolic or actual repetitive enactment of problem situations for the individual . . ."; (3) "They provide for the individual continuity of interest at various ages, in a culture filled with ambiguity of role function"; and (4) "They provide a transitional institution between work and play for the individual in his personal development, and for society." Men's play indeed has a positive serious function.

Yet the case studies remain in one's mind long after Beisser's conclusions have been forgotten. And what cannot be forgotten, above all else in the book, is the patient's fantasy with which Beisser concludes and which he takes to be

a grotesque metaphor of contemporary life in which reality is elusive. . . . He [the patient] pictures a family—father, mother, and children—sitting motionless in a semidark room. They appear unaware of one another as their collective gaze is transfixed on the lighted TV screen before them. Without looking, their hands, holding forks, move mechanically upward to their mouths and down again from TV trays on which rest TV dinners. They do not taste the food they eat, and they appear entirely occupied with the picture on the lighted screen. On the screen is a family—father, mother, and children—sitting motionless in a semidark room. They appear unaware of one another as their collective gaze is transfixed on the lighted screen before them. . . .[26]

More than a half century separates the analyses of Claparède and Beisser. The four theories of play's serious functions which we have just reviewed diverge widely. During the period of the unsettled debates concerning the psychology of play there emerged an entirely different and a quite widely known psychology having to do with play and games: it is an analysis of serious everyday individual and social activities as if they were games. The most widely read author of such an analysis is ERIC BERNE, whose *Games People Play* (1964) was a leading best-seller for longer than two years. A more recent work which makes the same use of the "game" metaphor has been written by A. H. CHAPMAN, another American psychiatrist, whose work is titled, *Put-Offs and Come-Ons: Psychological Maneuvers and Stratagems* (1968).

Game, as Berne defines it, is as central to Chapman's observations and descriptions of "put-offs" and "come-ons" as it is to Berne's own "transactional analysis." "A game," Berne writes,

is an ongoing series of complementary ulterior transactions progressing to a well-defined, predictable outcome. Descriptively it is a recurring set of transactions, often repetitious, superficially plausible, with a concealed motivation; or, more colloquially, a series of moves with a snare, or "gimmick." Games are clearly differentiated from procedures, rituals, and pastimes [i.e., from other possible types of human interaction] by two chief characteristics: (1) Their ulterior quality and (2) the payoff. Procedures may be successful, rituals effective, and pastimes profitable, but all of them are by definition candid; they may involve contest, but not conflict, and the ending may be sensational, but it is not dramatic. Every game, on the other hand, is basically dishonest, and the outcome has a dramatic, as distinct from merely exciting, quality.[27]

The game-names Berne gives to serious, everyday human activities are suggestive and often self-explanatory: "Now I've Got You, You Son of a Bitch"; "Look How Hard I've Tried"; "Why Don't You—Yes But"; "Let's You and Him Fight"; "I'm Only Trying to Help You"; "They'll Be Glad They Knew Me"; etc. Chapman has added to the list: "Whine and Decline: A Maneuver"; "You Can Never Repay Me: A Strategem"; "Look What You Did to Our Child"; "Love Will Come Later"; "I'm Going to Help You Rear Your Children"; "I'm in Analysis, You Know"; etc.

Both Berne and Chapman utilize the "game" metaphor to analyze unfortunate ways of human behavior to the end of implying a healthful life "beyond games." This is apparent, for example, in Berne's section entitled "Beyond Games." It is apparent also in Chapman's dedication of his book "to the memory of a friend who shunned all maneuvers and stratagems." In the end, these men seem to be hoping for and indeed preaching a human morality which would lead man beyond the sort of gaminess about which not only they, but also Stephen Potter, spoke.[28]

The work of THOMAS SZASZ, an American psychiatrist, is less simplistic and more sophisticated. The Myth of Mental Illness (1961) develops a thesis that involves a central use of the "game" metaphor, but it resists moralizing about the game of life. Szasz resists preaching about the "games" people play because he acknowledges the complexity involved in different types of human activities, or as he terms it, in "the hierarchy of games." Szasz writes: "Men are constantly engaged in behavior involving complicated mixtures of various logical levels of games." [29]

It is important to note two things about Szasz's argument. The first is that the author is concerned to clarify what he takes to be a misunderstanding based on the use of the term "illness," which literally applies to bodily ailments and which metaphorically describes certain psychic states and human behavior patterns. To view man's mental state *as if* it were either well or ill is to force the treatment of human behavior into patterns resembling the medical treatment of the human body. Such a view of psychiatry leads to perplexities which Szasz outlines in detail, and it is based on a logical error: the fallacy of misplaced logical types (i.e., applying the categories of one realm to the understanding of a totally different realm). Mental illness, Szasz argues, is a myth, if understood literally.

The second important aspect of Szasz's work is his substitution of what he calls "the game-model of human behavior" for the misunderstood and highly problematic physical-body model. Szasz follows Mead and Piaget in describing the "game/play" metaphor. Then he applies it to complex human activity by reference to "rule following" in tennis. We quote him here at length in order properly to understand his use of the phrase "hierarchy of games":

This game, along with many others, is characterized, first of all, by a set of basic rules. . . . Beginning at the level of the basic rules—assuming, that is, the presence of players, equipment, and so forth—it is evident that there is much more to an actual, true-to-life tennis game than could be subsumed under the basic rules. This is simply because there is more than one way to play tennis while still adhering to the basic rules. The basic rules merely provide a minimal framework or structure within which there is considerable latitude. For example, one player might want to win at any cost; another might consider playing fairly as most important. . . . Each of these techniques imply rules specifying (1) that in order to play tennis one must follow rules A., B., and C. and (2) how one should conduct oneself while following these rules. The latter could be said to constitute the rules of "meta-tennis." . . . These might include rules concerning style, the tempo of the game, and others. . . . It is important to note now that the goals of the basic game and of the higher level game may come into conflict, although they need not necessarily do so.[30]

Thus, we see why Szasz says "men are constantly engaged in behavior involving complicated mixtures of various logical levels of games." This understanding and use of the "game" metaphor makes it difficult to suggest the possibility of life "beyond games." All life lies somewhere in the hierarchy of games because, by definition, we are presented here with a "rule-following" model of human behavior.

But this leads one step further in the psychology of games and play. If life is like a game which follows rules like, say, the rules of tennis, then the analysis of life as being like a game (in this case, psychiatry) is itself a metagame which follows metarules like, say, those of metatennis. Szasz nearly acknowledges this when in a later book (*Law, Liberty and Psychiatry,* 1963) he describes the legal profession as being understood as a game and as a metagame. And if law, then also why not psychiatry—including the psychiatry which describes human behavior and law as a game!

This is the third step. Psychology may analyze games and play as having a serious function. It may also analyze serious activities as having the quality of games and play. This we have seen. But in addition to these two possibilities, it may apply its analyses to themselves and go the third step of analyzing its analyses as themselves a bit of play. An especially noteworthy example of this third step is the result of a team study undertaken initially in 1952 at Stanford University. The team included GREGORY BATESON, DON JACKSON, JAY HALEY, and JOHN WEAKLAND. (It is no accident that the work of Thomas Szasz becomes the transition to this ultimate stage of game-theory in psychology; he indicates in a footnote his indebtedness to Bateson's work in the development of an under-standing of the hierarchy of games.)

Jay Haley expresses the "third step" in a definition of psycho-therapy which he wrote in a book entitled, *Strategies of Psycho-therapy* (1963): "The structure of psychotherapy is a peculiar mixture of play and dead seriousness. It is a kind of game in which the participants maneuver each other; yet it is defined as the very essence of real life." [31] It is clear from a humorous "epilogue" in this "serious" textbook on psychotherapy that the author, himself involved "seriously" in the psychotherapeutic profession, is fully aware of the effect of allowing the "game" metaphor its vertiginous function, a function of implying a certain gaminess in the very use of the "game" term and a function, further, of implying a certain playfulness precisely at the point of the use of the "play" term. Haley's epilogic humor develops as a result of speaking of the process of psychotherapy in the terminology of Stephen Potter's "one-upmanship":

Psychoanalysis . . . is a dynamic psychological process involving two people, a patient and a psychoanalyst, during which the patient insists that the analyst be one-up while desperately trying to place him one-down, and the analyst insists that the patient remain one-down in order to help him learn to become one-up. The goal of the relation-ship is the amicable separation of analyst and patient. . . .

Although the many ways of handling patients learned by the analyst cannot be listed here, a few general principles can be mentioned. Inevitably a patient entering analysis begins to use ploys which have placed him one-up in previous relationships (this is called a "neurotic pattern"). The analyst learns to devastate these maneuvers of the patient. A simple way, for example, is to respond inappropriately to what the patient says. This places the patient in doubt about every-thing he has learned in previous relationships. . . . The analyst may say, "I wonder if that's *really* what you're feeling." The use of "really" is standard in analytic practice. It implies that the patient has motivations of which he is not aware. Anyone feels shaken, and therefore one-down, when this suspicion is placed in his mind.

Doubt is related to the "unconscious ploy," an early development in psychoanalysis. This ploy is often considered the heart of analysis since it is the most effective way of making the patient unsure of himself. Early in an analysis the skilled analyst points out to the patient that he (the patient) has unconscious processes operating and is deluding himself if he thinks he really knows what he is saying. . . . For example, the patient may cheerfully describe what a fine time he had with his girl friend, hoping to arouse some jealousy (a one-down emotion) in the analyst. The appropriate reply for the analyst is, "I wonder what that girl *really* means to you." This raises doubt in the patient whether he is having intercourse with a girl named Susy or an unconscious symbol. . . .

Ultimately a remarkable thing happens. The patient rather casually tries to get one-up, the analyst places him one-down, and the patient does not become disturbed by this. He has reached a point where he does not *really* care whether the analyst is in control of the relationship or whether he is in control. In other words, he is cured. The analyst then dismisses him, timing this maneuver just before the patient is ready to announce that he is leaving. Turning to his waiting list, the analyst invites in another patient who, by definition, is someone compelled to struggle to be one-up and disturbed if he is placed one-down. And so goes the day's work in the difficult art of psychoanalysis.[32]

Haley's views and his book were born, to a great extent, out of his participation in the Bateson-Jackson-Haley-Weakland research team. This team, working from 1952 to 1962 at the Veterans Administration Hospital and Stanford University in Palo Alto, California, were developing "the double-bind theory" of schizophrenia. The philosophical basis of their research was already spelled out in *Communication: The Social Matrix of Psychiatry* (1951), a book that Bateson wrote in collaboration with Jurgen Ruesch. But it was not until Bateson visited the Fleishhacker Zoo in San Francisco a year after the book's publication that the real impetus for the research was felt. Bateson describes his visit: "I saw two young monkeys *playing*, i.e., engaged in an interactive sequence of which the unit actions or signals were similar to but not the same as those of combat. It was evident, even to the human observer, that the sequence as a whole was not combat, and evident to the human observer that to the participant monkeys this was 'not combat.' Now, this phenomenon, play," Bateson deduces, "could only occur if the participant organisms were capable of some degree of meta-communication, i.e., of exchanging signals which would carry the message 'this is play.'"[33]

Like the metagame and metarules of Thomas Szasz's tennis match, the Fleishhacker monkeys' activities imply a hierarchy of games and rules with their not-to-be-confused hierarchies of logic. When the rules and the games are confused, i.e., when the rules of one level are applied to the game of another level, the result is a double bind, as for example in the famous philosophical conundrum, "Epimenides the Cretan said: 'All Cretans are liars.'" The double bind is as follows: If Epimenides' statement is true, it is false; and if false, then also true. The Palo Alto research team found this sort of double-bind communication to be characteristic of much everyday human interaction. When a person is unable to separate the levels (games) of man's thinking and feeling with their corresponding logics (rules), then he is placed in a psychological situation that is likely to end in psychic crisis. Some of the ways out of double-bind situations that the researchers found to be especially useful are humor,[34] play,[35] and psychotherapy. The latter, therefore, is easily identified as having a play-function.

All this is of course like saying that some monkey business in a zoo gives insight into human "monkey business" (human conflict), which in its turn is turned into human health by more "monkey business" (psychotherapy), which may be called "meta-monkey-business." Or perhaps we should say "monkey shines!"

In the double-bind teamwork the game/play metaphor reaches

its most complete form in the discipline of psychology. Analysis of play as having a serious function and analysis of serious human activity as having a playful function are viewed as applying also to those analyses themselves. The psychology of play may itself be viewed as a bit of play; the psychology of the games people play, far from transcending game-playing, may be thought of as just another game played at a different "level" of the hierarchy of self-consciousness. Our review has come full circle. Yet the review of psychologies of play would be totally remiss if it did not acknowledge the relatedness of all these different and sometimes differing theories to the central Freudian ideas about play.

FRANZ ALEXANDER, a Los Angeles psychiatrist, read a paper to a 1955 American Psychological Association meeting in which he reviewed the Freudian ideas about the psychological function of play and in which he made his own further contribution to these ideas. The paper was subsequently published in *The Psychoanalytic Quarterly* (April, 1958) under the title, "A Contribution to the Theory of Play." Alexander observes that "the essential feature of play is that during true playfulness the solution of a problem is not imperative." Play, therefore, is a nonutilitarian form of behavior which is characterized by "pleasureable activity for its own sake." On the Freudian view this means that play has a libidinal basis in the self, i.e., it is based in a personal drive which can be satisfied only through bodily pleasure. This is not to say that play is not important to the individual. To the contrary, "playful, erotic activities," as Alexander puts it,

are primary in the ontogeny of each individual. They constitute the building stones which will be utilized later in integrated adult behavior. In playfulness, isolated faculties are practiced and perfected, although at the time they do not seem to serve any utilitarian function. . . . Play is one of the important sources (though not the only one) of man's culture-building faculty by which he changes the world according to his own image. It is paradoxical that when man through scientific knowledge has become so efficient in securing with little effort the basic necessities of life, he becomes so deadly serious and looks nostalgically at the creative centuries of the past during which he still had that time and the detachment necessary for play and creativity. In this paradox lies the secret of understanding the crisis of Western civilization.[36]

Other "neo-Freudians," if we may so term them, feel similarly. NORMAN O. BROWN (*Life against Death*, 1959) interprets man's everyday language and more especially the creative language of the poet as having a playful function. Brown understands this playful function to be at bottom erotic. It allows the fulfilling expression of repressed childhood wishes which for full satisfaction imply physical delights. HERBERT MARCUSE (*Eros and Civilization*, 1955) had argued before Brown that the civilizing aspects of culture (such as human speech) are best understood as play. He writes: "Play and display, as principles of civilization, imply not the transformation of labor but its complete subordination to the freely evolving potentialities of man and nature. The ideas of play and display now reveal their full distance from the values of productiveness and performance: play is *unproductive* and *useless* precisely because it cancels the repressive and exploitative traits of labor and leisure; it 'just plays' with the reality. But it also cancels their sublime traits—the 'higher values.' The desublimation of reason is just as essential a process in the emergence of a free culture as the self-sublimation of sensuousness."[37] ERIK ERIKSON, too, gives a Freudian interpretation of human play as being important and primary in the developmental process of man and civilization. He writes, in *Childhood and Society* (1950):

What is infantile play, then? . . . it is not the equivalent of adult play, . . . it is not recreation. The playing adult steps sideward into another reality; the playing child advances forward to new stages of mastery. I propose the theory that the child's play is the infantile form of the human ability to deal with experience by creating model situations and to master reality by experiment and planning. . . . It is in certain phases of his work that the adult projects past experience into dimensions which seem manageable. In the laboratory, on the stage, and on the drawing board, he relives the past and thus relieves leftover affects; in reconstructing the model situation, he redeems his failures and strengthens his hopes. He anticipates the future from the point of view of a corrected and shared past. No thinker can do more and no playing child less. As William Blake puts it: "The child's toys and the old man's reasons are the fruits of two seasons." [38]

Lying behind the work of Brown, Marcuse, and Erikson is, of course, SIGMUND FREUD'S own ideas about play. The principal sources of these ideas are to be found in an article, "The Relation of the Poet to Day-Dreaming," first published in the *Neue Revue*, 1, in 1908, and a book, *Beyond the Pleasure Principle*, published twenty years later.

In the book, Freud has as his purpose to explain how the serious thoughts and actions of an individual are motivated by and large by "the pleasure principle," i.e., "mental events" are set in motion by an unpleasurable tension and they have as their central purpose to arrive at a lowering of that tension. Freud felt that human tensions were at base a result of bodily repressions imposed by external forces on the individual in his childhood. This principle, Freud found, is easily demonstrated by observing the function of the play of children. Such observation results, therefore, not only in a demonstration of the function of the pleasure principle, but also in an explanation of the purpose of play.

Freud's observations about play, according to his own account, revolved around an experience he had had living for a short time in a household where there was a one-year-old boy who had the

disturbing habit of taking any small objects he could get hold of and throwing them away from him into a corner, under the bed, and so on, so that hunting for his toys and picking them up was often quite a business. As he did this, he gave vent to a loud, long-drawn-out "o-o-o-o," accompanied by an expression of interest and satisfaction. His mother and the writer of the present account [Freud] were agreed in thinking that this was not a mere interjection but represented the German word *fort* ["gone"]. I eventually realized that it was a game and that the only use he made of any of his toys was to play "gone" with them. One day I made an observation which confirmed my view. The child had a wooden reel with a piece of string tied round it. It never occurred to him to pull it along the floor behind him, for instance, and play at its being a carriage. What he did was to hold the reel by the string and very skillfully throw it over the edge of his curtained cot, so that it disappeared into it, at the same time uttering his expressive "o-o-o-." He then pulled the reel out of the cot again by the string and hailed its reappearance with a joyful *"da"* ["there"]. This, then, was the complete game—disappearance and return. As a rule one only witnessed its first act, which was repeated untiringly as a game in itself, though there is no doubt that the greater pleasure was attached to the second act.[39]

Freud interprets this bit of child's play as a dramatic representation of the "child's great cultural achievement": the renunciation of the satisfaction of his bodily instincts which he had made when he allowed his mother to leave him from time to time. He compensated, or so Freud argues, for her departure (a source of displeasure) by turning a passive situation over which he had no control into a game (a source of pleasure) in which he took an active part. "In the case we have been discussing," Freud concludes, "the child may, after all, only have been able to repeat his unpleasant experience in play because the repetition carried along with it a yield of pleasure of another sort but none the less a direct one." The new pleasure, a compensatory pleasure to be sure, is the repetition of something which has made a great impression; but it is a repetition so as to make the player the master of that situation. Play, therefore, functions to satisfy "the pleasure principle."

Freud did not limit his views on play to the play of children. Indeed, understanding the play of children becomes a clue to the proper understanding of the creative work of the adult artist (poet, sculptor, etc.). While this play-aesthetic is spoken of in *Beyond the Pleasure Principle*, the basis for it was carefully laid in the article on "The Relation of the Poet to Day-Dreaming," which had been written twenty years earlier.

In this article Freud shows the play-function of a child's day-dreams. Just as a child plays because he wishes to be grown-up, i.e., to be master of the situation, so the daydream fantasies of a young boy or girl is one of the forms this play takes. In his day-dreams, the child is the hero or master. Furthermore, just as a child plays because he desires to fulfill an unsatisfied wish for bodily pleasure, so also in his daydream fantasies he is able to satisfy precisely those wishes. Thus, an understanding of the function of play is basic to the proper understanding of a child's daydreams.

But once this is observed, another step is implied. The poet, novelist, or dramatist does the same thing as a child at play. He creates a world in his imagination. Like the child's play-world, it is characterized, not by its lack of seriousness, but by its lack of correspondence to external reality. The only difference between the childish daydreamer and the poet is that the former hides his pleasurable fantasies from others, while the latter displays his fantasies for others' pleasure. The reason for this, Freud supposes, is that if a child were to tell his daydreams they would not give us the pleasure that the poet's imaginings do. Freud says:

How the writer accomplishes this is his innermost secret; the essential *ars poetica* lies in the technique by which our feeling of repulsion is overcome, and this has certainly to do with those barriers erected between every individual being and all others. We can guess at two methods used in this technique. The writer softens the egotistical character of the day-dream by changes and disguises, and, he bribes us by the offer of a purely formal, that is, aesthetic, pleasure in the presentation of his phantasies. The increment of pleasure which is offered us in order to release yet greater pleasure arising from deeper sources in the mind is called an "incitement premium" or technically, "fore-pleasure." I am of the opinion that all the aesthetic pleasure we gain from the works of imaginative writers is of the same type as this "fore-pleasure," and that the true enjoyment of literature proceeds from the release of tensions in our minds.[40]

Literary Criticism and Literature   It becomes clear that Sigmund Freud provides a key to understanding the relation between theories of play in psychology and theories of play in literature where the self is the primary point of focus. Freud's 1908 article arouses the curiosity enough to inquire as to whether or not literary critics and men of letters themselves think of their serious work *as* play. Not only is it possible to find such analyses among literary critics, but what is more compelling is the number of writers in the twentieth century who write serious works *about* play, i.e., using the play of children and adults as central metaphors in their poems, plays, and stories. There *is* evidence that men of letters are, in the most serious moments of their vocation, *at play*.

In the August 29, 1964, issue of *Saturday Review*, American poet and critic JOHN CIARDI wrote an article entitled, "Adam and Eve and the Third Son." Ciardi's words, here greatly abridged, speak eloquently for themselves:

> The poet is no sermonizer. To those who speak the language it may even seem clear that he has no interest in thinking. The poet, simply enough, is playing. His toys are words, images, rhythms, and forms. His game is to make his toys dance and perform all sorts of attitudes. He doesn't really much care what sort of dance it turns out to be or what sort of attitude his poems perform, though as he grows more and more practiced, he finds that there are certain dances and attitudes for which he has a special knack and to which he is specially drawn. . . . For the poet the goal is, as Peter Viereck once put it, "The ideas, the tall ideas *dancing*. . . ."

"Don't you know the world must be played for?" says the poet. "Were I to become as literal as you are, or as moral as you like to make me, I'd never have any fun, and I'd never stumble on a graceful error. What do you take me for, a preacher? . . .

"Forget the subject. [The poet is still speaking.] Meet me in the performance of the subject. In the idiom, in the images, in the rhythms, in the total structure. Meet me there, allow me my kind of play, and you will find that I can give you back your real variousness.

"Yes, . . . I do have a vision: the vision that you waste yourselves in conforming to your own overnarrowed images of yourselves. I need no vision to tell me you are much more various than you think you are. For I have been all of you and the father and mother of all of you and the keeper and shaper of the total legend in which you live. Except that you will not live in it totally, because you blind yourselves with the literal, and you call your literalness 'ideas.'

"I do not deal in ideas but in experiences. I must make illusions for you. I must make something happen, and it must be *as if* it is happening to you. Every *as if* experience you try on is another way of seeing yourselves. I must lead you to feel *as if* you were a child, a lover, a murderer, a dancer, a coward. For only as you try on all your possibilities vicariously can you come to know yourself.

"But you will be able to try them on if I only *tell you about them*. . . . I must make you feel them *as if* they were happening to you. And to do that, I must play my games.

"I am not even sure . . . that I play my games for you at all. I think I would play them if I were the last man alive. If I am in any way your benefactor, the benefaction is an accident. I play the games that let me write poems because I find that writing the poem is a better way of living than not writing it. Because I am happiest when I find myself winning a hard game with myself." [41]

So it is that Ciardi, a poet, speaks about the poet, while imagining himself, in his speaking, to be a poet. And Ciardi is not alone. The German novelist THOMAS MANN, writing in an address on Freud and the future, once said: "The artist's eye has a mythical slant upon life which makes life look like a farce, like a theatrical performance, a prescribed feast, like a Punch-and-Judy epic, wherein mythical character-puppets reel off a plot abiding from past time and now again present in a jest." Then commenting on his own novel, *Joseph and His Brothers,* Mann admitted: "The Joseph of the novel is an artist, playing with his *imitatio dei* upon the unconscious string."[42]

This is not only the view of Ciardi and Mann but also of W. H. AUDEN. Auden has written at length about "games" in an essay called "Dingley Dell and the Fleet." But two paragraphs from other sources will perhaps better make the point about the artist as player. The first is from Auden's "The Shield of Perseus" and the second is from his "The Poet and the City."

The only two occupations which are intrinsically serious are the two which do not call for any particular natural gifts, namely, unskilled manual labor and the priesthood. . . . Any unskilled laborer and any priest is interchangeable with every other. Any old porter can carry my bag, any trumpery priest absolve me of a mortal sin. One cannot say of an unskilled laborer or of a priest that one is better or worse than another [a characteristic essential to the player of games]; one can only say, in the case of the laborer, that he is employed, in the case of the priest, that he has been ordained. Of all other occupations, one must say that, in themselves, they are frivolous. [That is, they have the quality of games.][43]

If a poet meets an illiterate peasant, they may not be able to say much to each other, but if they both meet a public official, they share the same feeling of suspicion; neither will trust one further than he can throw a grand piano. If they enter a government building, both share the same feeling of apprehension; perhaps they will never get out again. Whatever the cultural differences between them, they both sniff in any official world the smell of an unreality in which persons are treated as statistics. The peasant may play cards in the evening while the poet writes verses, but there is one political principle to which they both subscribe, namely, that among the half dozen or so things for which a man of honor should be prepared, if necessary, to die, the right to play, the right to frivolity, is not the least.[44]

Auden, Mann, and Ciardi are pointing to what Yale professor of comparative literature, Geoffrey H. Hartmann, has called "the present, almost universal, acceptance of the element of playfulness in art."[45] And indeed, they seem supported in their views by the many works of contemporary literature in which the game/play metaphor is central. The works are too numerous to review and interpret here. That would take an entire book in itself. The authors mentioned on the following pages, therefore, are displayed as a representative sampling of the field.

Pirandello and Rilke should be mentioned first. The former utilized the "game" image as the central metaphor of one of his early plays. Some of the latter's poems utilized the term "play." However, it is not just because the words "game" and "play" are dominant in their literatures that these two writers are important in our review but, rather, because they used these terms at the turn of this century in ways which were soon to become important to the men of letters who followed them. They represent the beginning of the importance of the metaphor in contemporary literature; their work is primary.

LUIGI PIRANDELLO was an Italian dramatist and short-story writer. His play, *The Rules of the Game*, was published in 1919. Its hero, Leone, is dramatized as a man who has learned "every move in the game." "What game?" "Why . . . this one. The whole game—of life." Yet curiously enough, Leone's mastery of the "game" consists not in the mastery of an activity, but in the mastery of passivity. He "lets be." He allows his wife to have a lover. He allows his wife's lover to have his every wish, even to the point of giving in to the lover's wish to engage him in a duel, a duel which the lover is bound to win because of his superior skill with a pistol. Yet, ironically and absurdly, far from being *done in* by his philosophy of life, Leone *survives* in a marvelously theatrical ending. Leone masters the playing of the game of life and, paradoxically, that mastery consists in playing not-playing. Perhaps this is not too unlike Eric Berne's play "beyond games." In any event it is the only way, as Pirandello says, "to come through unscathed."

RAINER MARIA RILKE, a German poet, was also concerned to discover a way "to come through unscathed," or, as he put it in more positive terms, to achieve an "existence [that is] enchanted" (*das Dasein verzaubert*). And he, like Pirandello, sought the way to this authentic existence through the avoidance of the intensity of seriousness, the avoidance of "passion" and of the "rash song." Rilke sought, rather, for the human existence which is a lyrical song (*Gesang ist Dasein*), the song which is "easy for gods" (*Für den Gott ein Leichtes*). Such life would be

A Play of pure forces
that no one touches unless he kneels and admires;

it would be a life which is

Not less than the gentle secret perception
that overcomes us silently within,
Like a quietly playing child of an infinite conception.[46]

The authentic self, for Rilke, as for Pirandello, may be expressed through the metaphor of "play." Just how important this metaphor becomes to Rilke is perhaps nowhere better seen than in his fourth *Duino Elegy* (published in 1922):

When I'm in the humor to watch the marionettes, no,
But to gaze so hard that at last, to balance my gazing,
an angel must come as a player to quicken the puppet.
Angel and marionette: then at last there's a show.

Then is rejoined what we by our being here
have always sundered. Then first from our seasons arises
the circle of full transformation. Above and beyond us
the angel is playing. Look: must not the dying
guess how full of subterfuge is all we achieve here?
Nothing is anything. Oh, hours of childhood,
when behind the symbols was more than merely the past,
and before us was not the future. Sure, we were growing,
and often we strove to grow up sooner, half
for the sake of those who had nothing but being grown-up.
Yet we were content in our going alone
with things that last, and we stood there in the breach
between the world and the plaything, on a place
founded from the first for a pure event.[47]

Thus begins the use of the game/play metaphor in twentieth-century Western literature. If these beginning works unequivocally utilize the words "game" and "play" as metaphors of authentic selfhood, the game/play literature which was to follow exploited the complexity and ambiguity of the words.

For example, HERMANN HESSE's Nobel Prize-winning novel, *Das Glasperlenspiel* (1945)—a work which was given the Latin title, *Magister Ludi* ("The Game Master"), for its English version—pictures a future society in which there lives an aristocratic hierarchy of men. The elite subsociety is called the Castellian Order. This order is the last refuge of full humanity in a civilization that is perishing in the barren solemnity of a purely utilitarian view of life. The members of the order, these players of the Bead Game (*das Glasperlenspiel*), are participants in lighthearted, carefree play. Their training consists in the mastery of the Game, which has as its purpose the integration of former knowledge, in both the arts and sciences, so that a holistic scheme of meaning results. The Magister Ludi is the man who can integrate all knowledge by the manipulation of the rules of all knowledge-games into harmonic juxtaposition.[48]

It would seem that Hesse is duplicating the Rilkean and Piran-
dellean use of the game/play metaphor. It would seem that man-
the-player (*Homo ludens*) is presented as the ideal man of the
future. It would seem that the man who has mastered the game
(the Magister Ludi) is the paradigm of authentic selfhood. Yet it
is not at all clear in Hesse's novel that this is the "message." The
ambiguity of "playing the game" enters the plot when the hero
of the novel, Joseph Knecht, a man who spent his entire life striving
for and achieving the ideal of Magister Ludi, decides in the end
to leave the Castellian Order. Knecht slowly discovers that the
game/play ideal does not fully satisfy him because it distances him
from the everyday life of the common man.

In the works of other writers, too, the game/play metaphor
functions as a dramatic symbolization of the complexity and
ambiguity of authentic selfhood. This is the case even in works
for which the metaphor is less central than in *Magister Ludi*. Some
few examples will make the point.

The drama of the French writer JEAN GENET has been called
a "game of mirrors" by critic Martin Esslin.[49] Justification for the
game-of-mirrors description can easily be provided by recalling
the famous scene from Genet's play, *The Balcony* (1958), which
involves a conversation between the Chief of Police and the mistress of a brothel.

> *Irma:* Do you still insist on keeping up the game? No, no, don't be
> impatient. Aren't you tired of it?
>
> *The Chief of Police:* But . . . What do you mean? In a little while
> I'll be going home.
>
> *Irma:* If you can. If the rebellion leaves you free to go.
>
> *The Chief of Police:* Irma, you're mad. Or you're acting as if you were.
> The rebellion itself is a game. From here you can't see anything
> of the outside, but every rebel is playing a game. And he loves
> his game.

Irma: But supposing they let themselves be carried beyond the game? I mean if they get so involved in it that they destroy and replace everything. Yes, yes, I know, there's always the false detail that reminds them that at a certain moment, at a certain point in the drama, they have to stop, and even withdraw. . . . But what if they're so carried away by passion that they no longer recognize anything and leap, without realizing it, into . . .

The Chief of Police: You mean, into reality? What of it? Let them try. I do as they do, I penetrate right into the reality that the game offers us, and since I have the upper hand, it's I who score.

Irma: They'll be stronger than you.

The Chief of Police: Why do you say "they'll be"? Don't I have treasures invested, a thousand resources? All right, enough of that. Are you or aren't you the mistress of a house of illusions? You are. Good. If I come to your place, it's to find satisfaction in your mirrors and their trickery.[50]

This is a bit reminiscent of a scene from *Rosencrantz and Guildenstern Are Dead* (1967). This play by TOM STOPPARD begins with the two title characters playing a game of "heads or tails" and, at the same time, speculating on probabilities: "The law of averages, if I have got this right, means that if six monkeys were thrown up in the air for long enough they would land on their tails about as often as they would land on their——."[51]

And the play ends with the two men losing the "game of life" just as they do in Shakespeare's *Hamlet.* Guildenstern—dying— says:

Dying is not romantic, and death is not a game which will soon be over. . . . Dead is not anything . . . death is not . . . It's the absence of presence, nothing more.

·   ·   ·

There must have been a moment, at the beginning, where we could have said—no. But somehow we missed it.

·   ·   ·

Well, we'll know better next time. Now you see me, now you——.[52]

He disappears.

This is a bit different from KARL A. OLSSON's novel, *The God Game* (1968). Instead of the "game" ending with a murder, it begins with a suicide. Or, in the author's own words: "It begins with a suicide—the ultimate form of personal isolation—and it reveals, in the progression of its narrative, the withdrawal of man from man in a desperate game of self-sufficiency and subtle pride. This game is the God Game."

> "It's stupid. You can't be that for people unless you are God."
> "No, but can't you *imagine* that you are god for people without being god?"
> "Meaning?"
> "Meaning that's the game a lot of people play."[53]

At the end, the man of sinful pride (who incidentally is a clergyman) totally breaks *down* emotionally, mentally, and spiritually. But at the same time he breaks *through* the game of pretense, of self-sufficiency. He transcends the God Game; he becomes truly human.

Such transformation which moves man beyond life's ambiguous games is the theme, also, of EDWARD ALBEE's well-known play, *Who's Afraid of Virginia Woolf?* (1962). Psychological and sociological "fun and games," as Albee calls Act One, must be purged in order to resurrect authentic selfhood *not* characterized by gaminess. Games like "get the guests," "humiliate the host," "hump the hostess," etc., dramatize the vicious and vacuous nature of unconscious human relationships which unwittingly emerge when traditional principles of order—social, psychological, and religious—fail to sustain a sense of meaning in man's life.

> You take the trouble to construct a civilization . . . to . . . to build a society, based on the principles of . . . of principle . . . you endeavor to make communicable sense out of natural order, morality out of the unnatural disorder of man's mind . . . you make government and art, and realize that they are, must be, both the same . . . you bring things to the saddest of all points . . . to the point where there *is* something to lose . . . then all at once, through all the music, through all the sensible sounds of men building, attempting, comes the *Dies Irae*. And what is it? What does the trumpet sound? Up yours. I suppose there's justice to it, after all the years. . . . Up yours.[54]

The *Dies Irae* requiem must be sung, not only to bury the failing models of morality and wisdom, but also—as at the very end of the play—to bury the vicious and vacuous games that emerge during such failure. For, though being deprived of games comes as a terrifying trauma (as indeed it does to Albee's Martha and Olsson's David), it also purges and exorcizes the demons which rush in when the gods and their order retire.

It is a short step from the Albeean use of the "game" term to the use made by two men for whom, more than any other than perhaps Hermann Hesse, the metaphor has central significance. The writers are Argentinian-French novelist JULIO CORTÁZAR and Irish-French dramatist SAMUEL BECKETT. Their special importance in this review is seen in the similarity of, and yet also the significant difference between, the former's *Final del Juego* (*End of the Game*, 1966) and the latter's *Fin de Partie* (*Endgame*, 1958).

Beckett's use of the "game" metaphor in his 1958 play is neither arbitrary nor accidental. He had played with the term earlier in perhaps his most well-known work, *En Attendant Godot* (*Waiting for Godot,* 1953). One of the characters, whose name is Lucky (!) and who is otherwise totally mute during the action, has a single stream-of-consciousness speech in the middle of the drama. The speech, not too unlike George's *Dies Irae* speech in the Albee play, proclaims the end of an age in Western civilization.

Given the existence as uttered forth in the public works of Puncher and Wattmann of a personal God quaquaquaqua with white beard quaquaquaqua outside time without extension who from the heights of divine apathia divine athambia divine aphasia loves us dearly with some exceptions for reasons unknown but time will tell and suffers like the divine Miranda with those who for reasons unknown but time will tell are plunged in torment plunged in fire whose fire flames if that continues and who can doubt it will fire the firmament that is to say blast hell to heaven so blue still and calm so calm with a calm which even though intermittent is better than nothing but not so fast and considering what is more that as a result of the labors left unfinished crowned by the Acacacacademy of Anthropopopometry of Essy-in-Possy of Testew and Cunard it is established beyond all doubt all other doubt than that which clings to the labors of men that as a result of the labors unfinished of Testew and Cunard it is established as hereinafter but not so fast for reasons unknown that as a result of the public works of Puncher and Wattmann it is established beyond all doubt that in view of the labors of Fartov and Belcher left unfinished for reasons unknown of Testew and Cunard left unfinished it is established what many deny that man in Essy that man in short that man in brief in spite of the strides of alimentation and defecation wastes and pines wastes and pines and concurrently simultaneously what is more for reasons unknown in spite of the strides of physical culture that practice of sports such as tennis football running cycling swimming flying floating riding gliding conating camogie skating tennis of all kinds dying flying sports of all sorts autumn summer winter winter tennis of all kinds hockey of all sorts penicilline and succedanea in a word I resume flying gliding golf over nine and eighteen holes tennis of all sorts in a word for reasons unknown in

Feckham Peckham Fulham Clapham namely concurrently simultaneously what is more for reasons unknown but time will tell fades. . . .[55]

There is an expanding consciousness in this monologue of the
absurdity of man's attempt to master the games of life in a cultural
context which is fading and which, therefore, cannot support
meaning-systems which might give human significance to these
life-games.

It comes as no surprise, then, when five years later the author
of *Waiting for Godot* expands the metaphor of this speech into
an entire play and calls it *Endgame*. The implications of Lucky's
speech are fully explored. What sort of humanity is possible when
civilization has reached the end of the game? Two of the characters
spend the duration of the play in trash cans. Two others (named
Clov and Hamm) are totally dependent upon each other for sur-
vival and they fail, over and over again, as they try desperately
to construct a story of their past which might give a clue to their
future meaning. Clov, at one point, implores Hamm with the
words: "Let's stop playing!" But a little later Hamm indicates that
in spite of the absence of systems of meaning to support their
existence ("Old endgame lost of old, play and lose and have done
with losing") they must and they will continue to quest for and
celebrate the human enterprise ("Since that's the way we're playing it . . . let's play it that way . . . and speak no more about
it . . . speak no more. Old stancher! You . . . remain."). And this
is the way the play, the *Endgame*, ends. It is a dramatic symbolization of the contemporary complexities of serious human activities
of meaning expressed through the metaphor of "game."

Cortázar does just the opposite with his story, *End of the Game*.
He achieves a poetic expression of the games of children which
symbolize the complexities of serious adult meaning. Beckett
writes about seriousness as if it were a game; Cortázar, about a
game as if it were serious.

End of the Game has counterpoints in others of Cortázar's works, just as *Endgame* has prefiguration in Beckett's *Waiting for Godot.* In 1960 Cortázar published an important novel, *Los Premios (The Winners)*, which focuses the reader's attention on the ambiguity of "winning" a game. It raises the possibility that some men may win by losing, just as it is more obvious that some may lose by winning. The plot of *The Winners* treats a journey, a supposedly festive and luxurious cruise, which "the winners" have become entitled to by virtue of their winning a lottery. But the prize which comes from winning seems ambiguous at the beginning—

Lopez suddenly found it strange that the Tourist Lottery should ever have seemed unreasonable to him. Only because of his long observance of Buenos Aires—not to say more than that, to get metaphysical—was he able to accept as reasonable the spectacle that surrounded and included him. The most chaotic hypothesis of chaos paled before this confusion: ninety-two degrees in the shade, arrivals and departures, marches and countermarches, hats and brief cases, policemen and five-o'clock editions, buses and beers, all crammed into every fraction of every second and vertiginously transforming the following fraction of a second. Now the woman in the red skirt and the man in the checked jacket were about to pass one another, they were two pavement squares apart, at that same moment Dr. Restelli was bringing beer to his mouth, and the lovely (she really was) girl was taking out her lipstick. Now the two pedestrians were back to back, the glass was slowly lowered, and the lipstick was writing the eternal curved word. Who would have the nerve to think the lottery was strange?[56]

If the content of a game's ambiguity was mastered in *The Winners,* Cortázar matched this with a mastery of form in a second novel which continued the "game" terminology. Its Spanish title was *Rayuela;* English, *Hopscotch.* And it was published first in 1963.

The content of *Hopscotch* is a "game" of hopscotching from Paris to Buenos Aires in quest of love and, more broadly, life's meaning. And this content occasionally employs observations on a quite actual and literal hopscotch game—as in the following passage:

> . . . the harmony lasted incredibly long, there were no words that could answer the goodness of those two down there below, looking at him and talking to him from the hopscotch, because Talita had stopped in square three without realizing it, and Traveler had one foot in six, so that the only thing left to do was to move his right hand a little in a timid salute and stay there looking at La Maga, at Manú, telling himself that there was some meeting after all, even though it might only last just for that terribly sweet instant in which the best thing without any doubt at all would be to lean over just a little bit farther out and let himself go. . . .[57]

Though there is this interesting meeting of hopscotch literally understood and "hopscotch" as a metaphor of the quest for life's meaning, the major accomplishment of the novel lies in the meeting of literal *and* metaphoric content, on the one hand, with style and format, on the other. The book has 155 chapter divisions. But the author explains in an introductory "table of instructions" that the novel may be read in various ways. It may be read the way one normally reads a novel, proceeding consecutively from Chapter 1, in which case, the author informs us, the end of the novel is at Chapter 56. The rest may be ignored. Or if one prefers, he may begin reading with Chapter 73 and follow the instructions at the end of each chapter as to what should be read next: e.g., 73 - 1 - 2 - 116 - 3 - 84 - etc. It may even be, the reader suspects, that he may "hopscotch" through *Hopscotch*'s literal and metaphoric hopscotches in whatever route is best for his own quest—his own quest for meaning in life and for meaning in this novel—which would ultimately be the same. The novel is itself the game it is about! Hence, the following segment from the next to last (?) chapter, seems to be about itself:

> . . . a few people can approach those attempts without thinking that they're some new literary game. *Benissimo*. Worst of all, there is so much missing and he would die without having finished the game.
>
> "The twenty-fifth move, the blacks give up," Morelli said, throwing his head back. Suddenly he seemed much older. "It's too bad, the game is just getting interesting. Is it true that there is an Indian chess game with sixty pieces on each side?"
>
> "It's possible," Oliveira said. "The infinite game."
>
> "The one who conquers the center wins. From that point he dominates all possibilities, and it's senseless for his adversary to insist on continuing the play. But the center might be in some side square, or even off the board."
>
> "Or in a vest pocket."[58]

In *End of the Game* three children discover "the center." And in discovering it they become transformed from the delightful innocence of childhood into the exciting, but not always so delightful, realism of maturity. The three children, one of them crippled and distorted in physique, had invented a game which they called Statues and Attitudes. One of them, chosen by chance, would strike the pose either of a statue (e.g., the Venus de Milo) or of an attitude (e.g., Generosity, Piety, Sacrifice), depending again on a random selection, something like the lottery of *The Winners*. The props used for the game were stolen from their mother's jewel box. The scene of the game was in an open lot by a bend in the railroad tracks, the latter necessitated by the fact that such a game needs an audience for full enjoyment, or so they reasoned. A schoolboy who rode the same train each day became fascinated by the game he observed and, most especially, by the statues and attitudes of the lame girl, whose infirmity he did not notice because of the swiftness of his journey and because of the nature of the game itself. Until at last he came to visit the object of his affection, an affection which had grown as a result of his continued observation of her domination of the game. Letitia remained hidden in her room on the day of Ariel's visit. He was of course puzzled. But on the very next day Letitia performed the "most regal statue she'd ever done," with "her body [bent] backwards so far it scared us."

> I don't know why, the two of us started running at the same time to catch Letitia who was standing there, still with her eyes closed and enormous tears all down her face.[59]

Of course Ariel knew all, though the moment was brief. The girl of his affection was not what he thought. She had mastered the game; she was a "winner." And she had lost. It was the "end of the game." And the beginning of life.

The point seems to be—as indeed it seems to be in all the literature which employs the game/play metaphor—that in theories and expressions of the nature of the self, the disorder and conflict to be avoided *and* the order and harmony to be achieved may both be seen in the games and play of children.

Philosophy Recent philosophers of all sorts have been engaged in singing an Albeean sort of *Dies Irae* over the bodies of former traditional metaphysics. Both linguistic analytic philosophy and existential phenomenology, the two dominant versions of contemporary philosophical studies, have attempted to get behind the meanings of traditional philosophical statements so as to make them relevant to the advances in mathematics and science, on the one hand, and contemporary existence, on the other. And though these two movements are in many ways diverse, they have both found useful, just as have the social and the psychological theorists, the metaphors of "game" and "play."

In 1952, the German philosopher JOSEF PIEPER wrote a work whose English title is *Leisure: The Basis of Culture*. The argument of Pieper's book, as its title indicates, is not wholly unrelated to the thrust of Huizinga's *Homo Ludens*. Pieper is arguing for a change in attitude on the part of Western work-oriented man. As he says:

> Leisure, it must be clearly understood, is a mental and spiritual attitude—it is not simply the result of external factors, it is not the inevitable result of spare time, a holiday, a week-end or a vacation. It is, in the first place, an attitude of mind, a condition of the soul, and as such utterly contrary to the ideal of the "worker" in each and every one of the three aspects . . . : work as activity, as toil, as a social function.[60]

Pieper is proposing in the place of the common understanding of work as acti*vism*, "an attitude of non-activity, of inward calm, of silence; . . . not being 'busy,' but letting things happen." In the place of work's second ordinary aspect, work as toil, he proposes "an attitude of contemplative 'celebration.'" And, third, he proposes a nonutilitarian sense of "cheerful affirmation of his own being" in the place of the worker's fanatical tenseness about serving a social function. "However much strength it may give a man to work; the point of leisure is not to be a restorative, a pick-me-up, whether mental or physical; and though it gives new strength, mentally and physically, and spiritually too, that is not the point."[61] The point is not, therefore, that play is to be considered as a sort of Coca-Cola philosophy: "the pause that refreshes" *in order that* one may do more work. The point is rather that play and leisure, not seriousness and work, are the basis of culture. We who are inheritors of a Puritan and Victorian *faux pas* in attitudes have got it backwards. It is apparent, though Pieper makes his case logically and philosophically rather than historically and anthropologically, that his argument is integrally related to Huizinga's.

The difference between the two works, however, is that Pieper applies his argument about leisure and culture to the discipline of philosophy itself—that is, to the discipline which has enabled him to make the argument in the first place. In philosophizing, whether it be done after the manner of Plato or after the manner of Aristotle and Thomas Aquinas, man steps beyond the world of work and beyond the worker's attitude. Philosophical theorizing, Pieper's philosophical theory states, is (1) a nonactivity activity, a not being busy, a letting things happen; (2) it is a nonactivity activity also in the sense of being contemplative and celebrative of the wonder of being; and (3) it is nonutilitarian while at the same time being an "affirmation of being." "To philosophize," Pieper writes,

> is the purest form of *speculari*, of *theorein*, it means to look at reality purely receptively. . . . The assault upon philosophy's theoretical character is the historical road of philosophy's suicide. And that assault arises from the world's being seen more and more as mere raw material for human activity. . . . The loss of "theoria" means *eo ipso* the loss of the freedom of philosophy: philosophy then becomes a function within society, solely practical, and it must of course justify its existence and role among the functions of society; and finally, in spite of its name, it appears as a form of work or even of "labour." Whereas my thesis . . . is that the essence of "philosophizing" is that it transcends the world of work.[62]

For Josef Pieper, then, the philosophical analysis of serious culture as if it were based upon playful leisure leads to the understanding of philosophical analyses themselves to be most serious when they are themselves looked upon as bits of playful leisure.[63] Such play-theory in social and cultural philosophy does not stand alone. It has significant counterparts in the two most dominant branches of contemporary academic philosophy: linguistic analysis and existential phenomenology.

The German-English thinker LUDWIG WITTGENSTEIN is widely acknowledged to be the originator of that branch of philosophy called "linguistic analysis." And his popular, though controversial, game-theory of language is easily the most widely known use of the "game" metaphor in the discipline of philosophy.[64]

Those who knew him tell us that the notion of language-being-like-games occurred to Wittgenstein in the thirties as he was walking past a field where a game of English football was being played. As it developed, the idea included the notion of there being diverse types of language, each having its own set of rules ("logic"). In the *Philosophical Investigations,* a philosophical notebook written between the years 1933 and 1950, and published in 1953, two years after Wittgenstein's death, there is written:

> Consider for example the proceedings that we call "games." I mean board-games, card-games, ball games, Olympic games, and so on. What is common to them all?—Don't say: "There must be something common or they would not be called 'games'"—but *look* and *see* whether there is something common to all.—For if you look at them you will not see something that is common to *all,* but similarities, relationships, and a whole series of them at that. To repeat: don't think, but look![65]

This is to say that Wittgenstein did *not* develop a philosophy of language and meaning which theorized that the essence of language is the same as that of games; he did *not* think that he had discovered what language is *really* like (i.e., its metaphysical and ontological nature); rather, he utilized "game" as a metaphor to show what language is *like.*[66] "The concept of language-games as used in the *Investigations* cannot be warped into a static picture of games or spheres existing side by side or in layers or levels.

Continuing the metaphor, there are games within games within games. In the game of physics are the games of Newtonian mechanics and quantum mechanics, and each of these embodies other games. In psychology there is the theory-game and the therapy-game, and so on. Finally, there are games that can be described in no other way than as 'your' game and 'my' game."[67]

But if "game" is a metaphor in the philosophy of Wittgenstein there is a curiosity to be noted. Metaphors, as we noted earlier, are an intentional mixing of language games. "My love is a red, red rose." "Achilles is a lion in battle." "Language is a game." The rules ("logic") which apply properly to one game are intentionally misapplied to another game. Therefore, it follows that in using "game" *as a metaphor* in a philosophy of language for the purpose of clarifying the use of various logics and various languages, we are actually mixing logics and languages. Put baldly, Wittgenstein seems intentionally to be confusing things so as to get things clear! And this, it would seem, is precisely the basic insight of his idea of "language-games." "There is . . . nothing *a priori* wrong with crossing games. On the contrary, such a skillful use of language is *fun* (in an important sense of the idea) and advantageous to meaning."[68]

Philosophy is fun! Philosophy (including the linguistic analytic philosophy of language) is a game. And even more importantly, it is a metaphoric game. Few of Wittgenstein's followers have been willing to go this far; few of them have been willing to apply the implications of the "language-game" metaphor to their own language-game interpretations of language as a game. But the style of Wittgenstein's own philosophical writing seems to indicate the mentor's own willingness to see the *full* force of his own insights: he did not write ponderous and pedantic tomes of systematic philosophy; he wrote aphorisms! Playful little ploys aimed at the old metaphysical imperialism in philosophy! Gamelets and meta-games![69]

The scholars who populate the existential phenomenologist wing of contemporary philosophy are less inclined to affirm the possibility that their work is a sort of game. This is the case even for those whose work involves a central use of the metaphor of "play." Typical of their comments are: "To meditate on play is ostensibly not play." "The man who plays does not think, and the man who thinks does not play." [70] "A sound instinct in us holds all playing with ideas and concepts to be frivolous or silly or detestable, leading to a collapse of thinking." [71] "Only seriousness about play allows play wholly to be itself." [72] Nonetheless, in spite of their ultimate seriousness about play, or perhaps precisely because they do take play with such seriousness, some existential phenomenologists have become as fascinated, perhaps even more so than linguistic analysts, with the possibility that the "play" metaphor could contribute significantly to the human understanding of the structure and form of meaning in the contemporary world.

Two directions are noted in these philosophers: (1) a use of the concept of "play" for theorizing about the basic philosophical (i.e., ontological) nature of works of art and their place in human meaning—this is an "aesthetic-ontological" thrust which takes as its starting point the philosophies of Immanuel Kant and Friedrich Schiller; (2) a use of the concept of "play" for theorizing about the basic philosophical (i.e., ontological) nature of the world and man's place in it—this is a "cosmic-ontological" thrust which takes as its starting point the philosophies of Plato and, especially, Heraclitus and Nietzsche. The principal examples of each of these separate directions are to be found in the writings of two German philosophers: HANS-GEORG GADAMER and EUGEN FINK.

The title of a section from Gadamer's most important work, *Wahrheit und Methode* ("Truth and Method"), gives away his interest in the concept of play. The section is called *"Spiel als Leitfaden der ontologischen Explikation"* ("Play as the Leading Motif of the Ontological Explication"). The "ontological explication" that is being referred to is the ontology of the work of art. The concept of play is the basis for understanding the work of the artist. We have already encountered this argument from literary critics and we will encounter it again later from theological interpreters of the "religious" dimension of beauty in art. But Gadamer's analysis provides the idea with philosophical sophistication.

He repeats some portions of the arguments of German philosophers who have preceded him in an aesthetic of play, notably, FRIEDRICH J. J. BUYTENDIJK and THEODOR HAECKER. The former had written: "Animals and men play only with images. . . . The realm of play is the realm of the image and, therefore, the realm of possibility and imagination."[73] And Haecker had already said: "The man who cannot play with images is no artist; and he who cannot understand the play of imagery cannot understand art. . . . The freedom of play that we have in [an art-work's] images expresses itself freely as the freedom of play—not in any single image, but in the whole [of the art-work]—the freedom of play of a higher truth, namely, that of true creation."[74]

These two related ideas, i.e., that human play is a matter of creative imagination and that the creative artist is a player, are the basis for Gadamer's use of the metaphor of "play" in an ontology of aesthetics. Gadamer's own contribution to these ideas is to note that in order to avoid individualistic subjectivism in aesthetics according to which every artist's imaginative fantasies and every interpreter's playful criticism is as good as every other man's, it is necessary to focus on "the primacy of *play*" rather than on "the activity of the *player*." This is to say that a proper understanding of aesthetics should focus on the work of art rather than on the artist. And it is precisely the concept of "play" which demonstrates this otherwise not-so-obvious point.

So Gadamer writes: "The subject of play is not the player; it is rather that play comes through the players solely in the performance." "Whoever does not take play seriously is a spoilsport. The 'play' mode of being does not permit the player to be related to play as to an object. The player knows what play is and that what he does is 'mere play,' but he does not know that he 'knows' this [while in the act of playing]." So it is also in the art-work and for the artist: "When we speak of the experience of art in the context of 'play,' 'play' does not mean the condition or mind-set of creativity or enjoyment and, generally, not the freedom of subjectivity that is activated through play. Rather, it means the mode of being of the work of art itself."[75] For Gadamer, then, the concept of "play" enables him to construct a "phenomenological" aesthetic and to avoid the awkwardnesses of a theory of the interpretation of art which pictures art as the subjective and emotive frivolities of hyperimaginative individuals.

Eugen Fink is also eager to focus on the objectivity of "play" rather than on the activity of the player, or, as he enigmatically calls it, "the play without a player." His explanation is not much help: "The play of the world is the play of no one because it is only in itself that there are persons, men and gods."[76]

Perhaps these difficult phrases—"play without a player" and "the play of the world is the play of no one"—will be a bit more comprehensible if we first note what it is that concerns Fink. He feels strongly that the tradition in academic philosophy from Plato to Hegel, a more than two-thousand-year tradition, has gone astray by not focusing more on what is generally called "cosmology," the inquiry into the nature of the world. But it is not exactly "cosmology" in the traditional sense of the term that is Fink's concern. It is, rather, that he thinks that human meaning is best and indeed only understood as man is seen *in relation to the world*. When man and world are studied separately as being based in distinct essences or as being distinct substances, the dynamic quality of meaning is lost. The reason for the eclipsed focus on man in relation to world, or so Fink believes, is that as the history of

Western philosophy developed, more and more attention was given to another relationship, that of man and God. It is therefore this "theological character of metaphysics" that has obscured holistic concepts of meaning in philosophy.

What Fink intends to do is to call attention to another possibility of philosophical understanding. He wants to show that it is possible to conceive of personhood, including both man and God, under the heading of *world*. And the clue to this conception is to understand the world as "play," as playing itself out in structures of human meaning.

Fink, more than any other philosopher in the German phenomenological stream, sees what such a philosophical use of "play" may imply for the understanding of the task of philosophy itself. For in order to make his argument, he has built his case on the precedent of a philosopher who dates before Plato (Heraclitus) and one who comes after Hegel (Nietzsche). And both Heraclitus and Nietzsche philosophized, not only about play, but also playfully, i.e., in the mode of playful aphorisms. Therefore, Fink is no stranger to the argument that "play" is useful as a philosophical metaphor for the understanding of world. He thinks there is a possibility that philosophical understandings may themselves be "play" (including the philosophical understanding which sees the world as "play"). So he writes: "We are persuaded that a comprehensive interpretation of human play already presupposes an ecstatic overture to the world. . . . Is it not possible that . . . there may well be an authentic meditation, truly on play, which remains in the realm of play, which is held in the openness to the world that is informed by play? This question is not idly posed. . . ."[77] Indeed it is not. For Fink's own earlier book on play, *Oase des Glücks: Gedanken zu einer Ontologie des Spiels* (1957), is itself a brief, fifty-one-page lyric, which closes, after long quotations in defense of play by Nietzsche and Rilke, with these words: "Since this philosopher and this poet point towards the worth of the concept of play in such a profound and humane manner, we should also recall the words of another: we cannot enter the Kingdom of Heaven unless we become like little children."[78]

Mathematics   It is indeed an examination of the games of children (especially tic-tac-toe) that led contemporary mathematicians into the kingdom of game-theory. The games of adults (especially chess) have played an important role, too. For game-theory in mathematics is the systematic study of the principles ("logics") involved when decisions are made involving two or more decision-makers and when the decisions are in conflict situations (as in tic-tac-toe and chess). Hence, game-theory in mathematics is to games of strategy as probability-theory is to games of chance.

Game-theory and probability-theory differ widely, not only in their subject matters, but also in their origins. The latter came about as a result of solutions provided by the seventeenth-century theologian-mathematician Blaise Pascal to specific problems posed by a gambler acquaintance, Chevalier de Méré. Game-theory, on the other hand, was not devised so that men could win at chess, tic-tac-toe, and other two-person games. Game-theory stands very much in contrast to such practical considerations. Its main theorem was presented by John von Neumann at Göttingen, Germany, on December 7, 1926, as a speculative theory about the structural relationships which characterize "the formal aspect of rational decision." Therefore, as American mathematician Anatol Rapoport puts it, "'What is the best way to play Chess?' is not a game-theoretical question. On the other hand, 'Is there a best way to play Chess?' is a game-theoretical question."[79] Rapoport goes on:

> What distinguishes games from nongames from the point of view of game theory is not the seriousness or lack of seriousness of a situation, nor the attitudes of the participants, nor the nature of the acts and of the outcomes, but whether certain choices of actions and certain outcomes can be unambiguously defined, whether the consequences

of joint choices can be precisely specified, and whether the choosers have distinct preferences among the outcomes.[80]

There are two matters about mathematical game-theory which deserve the attention of this review. The first has to do with terminology. When confronted with a new theorem which treats "the formal aspect of rational decision," creative mathematicians did not choose to name it "decision-theory" or "choice-theory," names which would have paralleled the earlier name for the logic of chance determination (i.e., "probability-theory"). Instead, they called it "game-theory" and took the theory's models from tic-tac-toe and chess. The principles derived from such game models, according to the theory, might then potentially be reapplied to serious social, political, and moral decision-making. The implication of this terminological choice is clear: it is *not* that nongame activity becomes the basis for decision-making in games (as for example happens in Monopoly where serious business practices become the basis for playing a game); it is *rather* that the "rules" for decision-making in everyday, serious affairs are modeled on the logic of the literal games children and adults play.

But this is not the only item of importance for our review. Curiously—and this is the second point—game-theory in mathematics brings about a reversal in the thinking about the nature of the discipline of mathematics itself. Just as the introduction of the game/play metaphor into philosophy reformed the traditional imperialism of Platonic and Aristotelian logics, so in mathematics, this purest form of rational speculation, there occurs a reversal of intellectual dogmatism when the "game" ploy plays against its own playing. So Rapoport writes at the end of his book:

> The lesson to be derived [from game-theory in mathematics] is that many of our cherished notions about every problem having an "answer," about the existence of a "best" choice among a set of courses of action, about the power of rational analysis itself, must be relegated to the growing collection of shattered illusions. Rational analysis, for

all its inadequacy, is indeed the best instrument of cognition we have. But it often is at its best when it reveals to us the nature of the situation we find ourselves in, even though it may have nothing to tell us how we ought to behave in this situation. Too much depends on our choice of values, criteria, notions of what is "rational," and, last but by no means least, the sort of relationship and communication we establish with the other parties of the "game." These choices have nothing to do with the particular game we are playing. They are not *strategic* choices, i.e., choices rationalized in terms of advantages they bestow on us in a particular conflict. Rather they are choices which we made because of the way we view ourselves, and the world, including the other players. The great philosophical value of game-theory is in its power to reveal its own incompleteness. Game-theoretical analysis, if pursued to its completion, *perforce* leads us to consider other than strategic modes of thought.[81]

Theology   It is one thing to use "play" and "game" terminology to construct academic theories about nature, the social order, and the self, but it is an altogether different matter to speak of religious matters, indeed, of the gods and God himself, in these terms. It may seem to some even blasphemous. Of course, it *is* true that some contemporary studies of religion which have adopted the game/play metaphor are far from orthodox in their viewpoint. But what may seem surprising to some is the quite blatant fact that the greatest number and the finest quality of "game" and "play" theologies have been written by very orthodox scholars who themselves stand squarely in the front doors of the religious traditions they are interpreting. This is not to say that the metaphors of game and play do not have radical theological implications for the study of religion. Not at all. The implications are far-reaching as we shall see in Chapter 6. For now, however, we must get on with the task of reviewing both the orthodox and the not-so-orthodox examples of the use of the game/play metaphor in the field of theology.

Perhaps the least "orthodox" (from the perspective of Western Judeo-Christian academic theology) of serious attempts to utilize

the game/play metaphor in works on religion is a recent book by
ROBERT S. DEROPP. The book is called *The Master Game: Pathways
to Higher Consciousness beyond the Drug Experience* (1968). De-
Ropp urges his reader to "seek, above all, for a game worth playing.
Such is the advice of the oracle to modern man. Having found
the game, play it with intensity—play as if your life and sanity
depended on it. (They *do* depend on it.)"[82] DeRopp's book tells
what the most important game is (he calls it a metagame) and how
to play it.

The book cites game-theorists whom we have already reviewed,
notably Eric Berne, Thomas Szasz, and Hermann Hesse. But the
stress is very different from that of these men. The accent is foreign.
More specifically, it is Eastern. The Master Game is the game of
"full consciousness" or "real awakening" which Eastern mystics
of both Hindu and Buddhist slant (not to mention Western Jewish
and Christian mystics) have long known about. DeRopp categorizes
the games religious people play (and that includes all of us) as
Higher and Lower Games, or Metagames and Object Games. The
categorization is based on the games' aims. Charted, it looks
something like this.

Metagames and Object Games [83]

Game	Aim
Master Game	Awakening
Religion Game	Salvation
Science Game	Knowledge
Art Game	Beauty
Householder Game	Raise Family
No Game	No Aim
Hog in Trough	Wealth
Cock on Dunghill	Fame
Moloch Game	Glory or Victory

It is apparent from this chart that DeRopp considers the Master Game, which is "the only game really worth playing," to be a sort of Religion of religions, a practice of human meaning that takes the "best" (i.e., the mystical practices) from all religions and frees it from the traditional and now outmoded ecclesiastical frippery. DeRopp is providing modern man with a recipe book, a do-it-yourself secular religion.

He feels strongly about his program, as is obvious from statements like this one:

> The basic idea underlying all the great religions is that man is asleep, that he lives amid dreams and delusions, that he cuts himself off from the universal consciousness (the only meaningful definition of God) to crawl into the narrow shell of a personal ego. To emerge from this narrow shell, to regain union with the universal consciousness, to pass from the darkness of the ego-centered illusion into the light of the non-ego, this was the real aim of the Religion Game as defined by the great teachers, Jesus, Gautama, Krishna, Mahavira, Lao-tze and the Platonic Socrates. Among the Moslems this teaching was promulgated by the Sufis, who praised in their poems the delights of reunion with the Friend. To all these players, it was obvious that the Religion Game as played by the paid priests, with its shabby confidence tricks, promises, threats, persecutions and killings, was merely a hideous travesty of the real game.[84]

The remainder of the book consists of instructions for playing the Religion Game "as it was meant to be played," as opposed to the way it has been taught by church, synagogue, and temple. It is no surprise that the instructions for proper play are taken largely, as is the interpretation of "the basic idea underlying all the great religions," from certain mystical forms of Eastern religions, notably Vedanta Hinduism and Yoga.

ALAN WATTS is another and more widely known writer who has applied the traditional Vedanta notion of "play" to a general understanding of all religious consciousness. Watts, however, does not risk the dogmatic implications of making his books normative and practical sets of instructions. His books are more the disclosure of a "play" point of view than they are manuals of how to win at the game of life. In this way they are more instructive than is DeRopp's book for the academic study of religion. This is true even though the points of view are quite similar.

Watts teaches the reader the classical Vedanta view that the world is the result of the play of God. Attitudes of seriousness are therefore not in order. Rather, the proper attitude of reverence is to join in the joy of the game of God. In fact, the appropriate attitude for such a theology of play is indicated in the playful titles of Watts's works. The two that are most relevant to our review are: *Beyond Theology: The Art of Godmanship* (1964), and *The Book: On the Taboo against Knowing Who You Are* (1966). The arguments of these books are not really arguments at all, but ploys. The playfulness of the ploys is indicated by the following sample:

The insides of most Protestant churches resemble courthouses or town halls, and the focal point of their services is a serious exhortation from a man in a black gown. No golden light, no bells, incense, and candles. No mystery upon an altar or behind an iconostasis. But people brought up in this atmosphere seem to love it. It feels warm and folksy, and leads, on the one hand, to hospitals, prison reform, and votes for all, and, on the other, to sheer genius for drabness, plain cooking ungraced with wine, and constipation of the bright emotions—all of which are considered virtues. If I try to set aside the innate prejudices which I feel against this religion, I begin to marvel at the depth of its commitment to earnestness and ugliness. For there is a point at which certain types of ugliness become fascinating, where one feels drawn to going over them again and again, much as the tongue keeps fondling a hole in a tooth. . . .

. . . it does not seem to have occurred to most Christians that the means of grace might include trickery—that in his cure of souls the

Lord might use placebos, jokes, shocks, deceptions, and all kinds of indirect and surprising methods of outwitting men's wonderfully defended egocentricity. . . .[85]

Lest this sort of talk (and DeRopp's, too) seem a bit sacrilegious, we should quickly mention the names of two well-respected Christian theologians who stand squarely in the circle of Roman Catholic orthodoxy, but who, nonetheless, have much affinity to Watts and DeRopp. The names are DOM AELRED GRAHAM and FATHER HUGO RAHNER. The former is the head of the Benedictine Community in Portsmouth, Rhode Island, and, in that capacity, has written a book entitled *Zen Catholicism* (1963). In that work the "play" metaphor is used as a way of conceiving the practical ideal of a religious life. Graham's book, therefore, is not wholly unlike DeRopp's. Hugo Rahner, on the other hand, is a European Jesuit scholar who has written a more theoretical theological work whose basic understanding of religion turns on the "play" metaphor. The book, *Eutrapelie, Eine vergessene Tugend* (English title: *Man at Play*), was originally published in 1963 and contains a point of view not too unlike the works of Alan Watts, the main difference being simply that Rahner's source for a "play" theology is found—and this will be surprising to some—in the substantial tradition of the fathers and theologians of Western Christendom.

Though Graham's book has a practical orientation and Rahner's a theoretical one, both have the same basic thrust. The central point of *Zen Catholicism* is to be found in Chapter 7, whose title clearly reveals its point: "Playing God or Letting God Play?" In this chapter the author shows the important similarities between the disciplines of Zen Buddhist and Benedictine monks. He describes these disciplines in terms of "play and relaxation," "playfulness in mature years," "the value of casualness," "we are God's playthings," "the game of life," "the experience of God," etc. The essence of a deeply religious man is "not to initiate but to respond," not to be activist but accepting, not—in short—to play God but to let God play through man. The essence of man the religious animal (*Homo religiosus*) is best understood by defining man as a player (*Homo ludens*). This is Graham's point, and it is the theological anthropology of Rahner, too.

Man at Play is a title intended to convey an understanding of the religious ideal. Under that title, Rahner addresses himself to the notions of "the playing of God," "the playing of man," "the playing of the Church," "the heavenly dance"—

> In the last analysis there is a secret, a mystery, at the heart of every form of play, and [it is] that in it all, from the playing of children to the playing in heaven, there is one intent—the blessed seriousness of which, as Plato saw long ago, God alone is worthy. . . . There is a sacral secret at the root and in the flowering of all play: it is man's hope for another life taking visible form in gesture.
>
> To play is to yield oneself to a kind of magic, to enact to oneself the absolutely other, to pre-empt the future, to give the lie to the inconvenient world of fact. In play earthly realities become, of a sudden, things of the transient moment, presently left behind, then disposed of and buried in the past; the mind is prepared to accept the unimagined and incredible, to enter a world where different laws apply, to be relieved of all the weights that bear it down, to be free, kingly unfettered and divine. Man at play is reaching out—as has been said—for that superlative ease, in which even the body, freed from its earthly burden, moves to the effortless measures of a heavenly dance.[86]

—and Rahner ends the book with a chapter on "*eutrapelia,* the forgotten virtue."

Throughout the entire discussion the notions of man, church, and God as engaged in a marvelously and joyously graceful bit of play are thoroughly documented and underpinned by continual reference to the wealth of these same ideas as developed by theologians within the history of the very orthodox and traditional church. The book is in no way dilettantish, unless one means by this term what it originally meant (the Italian *dilettare* is literally translated "to enjoy"). Rahner's theology refocuses contemporary scholarship of the Christian religion on what has been so lacking in the overly serious and pedantic tomes of much past theology; it focuses on the true "enjoyment" and the delightful hilarity that is supposed properly to be the end of Christianity's salvific grace.

It is not Roman Catholic theology alone that has been attracted by the game/play terminology. Academicians in the Protestant wing of Christianity have focused their uses of the metaphor either in studies of the sociology of religion or in studies on the history of religions. The book *Religion and Leisure in America* (1964) by ROBERT LEE and the article "Leisure, Worship, and Play" (in *Crossroads*, March, 1966) by ELEANOR SHELTON MORRISON are fine examples of the former thrust. A doctoral dissertation, *Play and the Sacred: Toward a Theory of Religion as Play* (1964), and another article in *Crossroads*, "Religion and Play" (July-September, 1967), both by an assistant professor of theology at Union Theological Seminary in New York, ROBERT E. NEALE, are exceptionally fine examples of the latter.

In the sociological studies it is the problem of increasing leisure time that confronts the scholar of religion. By employing the game/play metaphor at a deeper and more spiritual level than it is usually understood, the scholar shows how to fight idleness with play. Lee, for example, draws on the analyses of play by Callois, Huizinga, and Pieper. This enables him to demonstrate a religious dimension to ordinary play which may then be appropriated as an attitude that might be utilized in grappling with unused leisure. Similarly, and also very much like Hugo Rahner, Eleanor Morrison argues:

Although adults attempt to compartmentalize children's lives into businesslike sections of work and play, children find ways of turning work into play. Life is whole to them, and good, like the creation according to the Genesis story. . . . Play and leisure seem native to children. . . . Unless worship bears connection with what we know to be native to children, it will tend to be sterile, stereotyped, and alien. Look well, therefore, to the meanings of leisure and play, for you may discover the seeds of worship as well.[87]

The historian of religions has a different purpose in employing the play metaphor. He is concerned to show what really constitutes the religious phenomenon which lies at the base of all specific religions; he has as his principal business to define the anatomy of *the sacred*. Robert Neale's work is a good example of such study where the play metaphor is used centrally. Neale says that his dissertation and article intend to be a religious psychology of human play; but in fact these works function as a close analysis of the evolution of religious consciousness in man, as a description of the phenomenon of the revelation of the holy or the sacred in relation to this religious consciousness, and as an argument for both the religious consciousness and the religious phenomenon to be viewed *sub specie ludi,* from the point of view of the category of play. Put in less technical language, Neale's accomplishment is to show (1) that man is basically a playing animal, (2) that religion is basically the playful response to God in ritual and myth-telling, and therefore (3) . . .

To have a playtime and playground with a story to tell and a game to play is to have a life of adventure that surpasses all description. . . . Whereas the worker anticipates or becomes disillusioned about "somewhere" and "sometime," the player lives a sanctified life. He does not alternately fight the world and escape from it as the profane worker does, nor does he usefully and abusively covenant with it as the magical worker does. Rather, the full adult adventurer is in communion with the world, demonstrating the love that is identical to that expressed by the gods in their creation of the world in the beginning. The paradise of the player is here and now. What happens to the child in play can happen to the adult. And when it does, paradise is present.[88]

The well-known Dutch historian of religions GERARDUS VAN DER LEEUW has, like Neale, linked the concept of play to an understanding of religious phenomena. His widely read *Religion in Essence and Manifestation* contains an example of this use of the play metaphor in the interpretation of religion. Yet van der Leeuw's major contribution to "play" theologizing occurs not in a history of religions or a sociology of religion study, not in a practical or theoretical theological treatise, but in a study of the religious dimensions of works of art. The book is entitled *Vom Heiligen in der Kunst* and has been published in English translation as *Sacred and Profane Beauty: The Holy in Art* (1963).

In this book van der Leeuw is concerned to offset an aesthetic which argues that "art is imitation." "Art is not an imitation of the movement of life," he argues. "Art has its own movement."[89] In searching for a substitute concept for imitation, the author discovers the metaphor of play. He defines dance, drama, pictorial arts, and music as a "game" and as "the play of men." But he goes beyond the aesthetics of play to a theological aesthetic of play. He warns man against taking himself "so seriously that he forgets that human life has the nature of a game," a flaw attributable to "fatal, mortal pride." And then he argues:

The meeting of God with man, of man with God, is holy play, *sacer ludus*. The theological nature of the dance . . . lies in movement; that of the drama, in movement and countermovement. God moved; he came down to earth. Then the puppets on earth moved also; or, if one prefers, the bones in the dry valley of Ezekiel. God began; we followed. For we are only "God's masques and costume balls," as

Luther says, or "God's toys," as Plato puts it. The most ancient drama, the drama that rules the world, is the drama of the meeting of God and man. God is the protagonist. We are only his antagonists. And we play a dangerous game, for we share this honor with the devil. . . .

Among primitive men, every game, even a game of chance, is a religious activity, a contact with invisible powers. . . . the concept of game ranks above that of seriousness. For seriousness tries to exclude the game, while the game can easily include seriousness. . . . For this reason, the game points beyond itself: downward, to the simple, ordinary rhythm of life; upward, to the highest forms of existence. . . . Play is the prerequisite for those forms of existence which strive toward a communion with the other, and finally for a meeting with God.[90]

"Play is the prerequisite." This is to say that play, literally understood, becomes a metaphor for the religious life in which there is a meeting, a covenant, between man and the Power that lies beyond him. And nowhere is this paradigmatic spirituality present more expressively than in the "play" of the dancer, the poet, the artist, and the musician. Aesthetics focusing on the category of play becomes a basis for theology.

At this point we begin to see the radical implications for theology of the game/play metaphor. This metaphor, with its aesthetic implications, has no use for theology that is unaesthetic (anesthetic), which is to say, unfeeling. "Play" theology will dethrone the theologies which have already dethroned our deities by burying them in hair-splitting logics and obfuscating logorrhea, profaning the joyful spirit of the religions that such theologies were so inappropriately attempting to explain. That "play" theology has opened the possibility of a radically new mode of writing about religion, a mode which is somehow more in the spirit of the thing it is attempting to articulate, is nowhere more apparent than in a potent little book whose subtitle is "A Play-Pray Book." We are thinking, of course, of the work of the former nun, SISTER MARY

CORITA, whose book is called *Footnotes and Headlines* (1967). Father Daniel Berrigan writes in the Introduction, "The first rule about any game is Throw the Rules Away." Sister Corita has done just that.

The book is a montage of aphorisms and images, of footnotes and headlines, of bright colors and bold types, of words written upside down and sideways, of—yes, above all—of puns.

> For a larger man to celebrate,
> more muscles are needed—someone needs to order
> the cake and champagne or the bread and
> wine and see that the musicians come. Someone needs
> to assess the contents of the cupboard—see that
> there are dishes and spoons and flowers and flags
> which are the extensions
> of man's inner equipment.

· · ·

> Someone's got to order the groceries.
> But if he only knows physical facts and knows no
> poetry or irony, he will be out of the celebration
> and only a drone. And the party will miss him
> and be less good or maybe not even go on.

· · ·

> Evil may be not seeing well enough
> so perhaps to become less evil we need only to see
> more   see what we didn't see before   and here every-
> body is in the game   things look different to
> different people depending on where they stand

· · ·

> games can restore life
> playing around with words
> taking them out of one context and putting them
> into another is a way of preserving or
> restoring their life.[91]

The application of the game/play terms to religious matters may indeed be a word game. But in such an academic theological game there might be discovered, not only the religious dimension in man's play, not only the playful dimension in man's religions, but "a way of preserving or restoring" the life of theologies which have been seen as irrelevant to modern experience and of the gods whose deaths have been recently announced.

Summary   This review of the academic use of "games" and "play" as theoretical metaphors has extended for many pages. What has it all shown?

First, we have seen a new interest in the fields of psychology, sociology, anthropology, and ethnology in analyzing children's games and the games and sports adults pursue in their leisure. This is simply to say that there is an initial curiosity about games and play—about their characteristics, their classifications, their important human functions—that was of little or no concern prior to the First World War.

Second, we have seen that this new interest and curiosity as to the meaning of games and play has been extended so that game-activity and the whole realm of play is not only viewed as having a serious purpose but is also viewed as being the basis for and a way of seeing all serious human endeavor. So, anthropological and ethnological theories have been advanced in which primitive societies were understood as being based in the human urge to play. Sociologists have pictured everyday social intercourse as if it were played out according to definite but often unarticulated rules of a social game. Psychologists have articulated for us the meaning of our individual play and ploys, both those we foist on others and those on which we hoist ourselves. Communication theorists have explained the intricacies of communication media on the model of game- and play-activity. Theologians have shown that our most sacred religious rituals may best be understood as men at play. Philosophers have analyzed our total human meaning on the basis of game and play functions. And mathematicians have developed a set-system of game-theory to the place that it may well be applicable to all of life's decisions. Indeed, contemporary academic disciplines have demonstrated clearly that in the university, as in everyday discourse, play's the thing.

Third, we have seen that sooner or later, while the academician is, as the saying goes, "doing his own thing," the theoretical use of the game/play metaphor rebounds on itself, i.e., it rebounds on the theoretical use of the game/play metaphor. It would seem that one of the impacts of game-theory on theoretical studies is to introduce into the academy a new awareness of the function and place of academic disciplines in the total social context. It would seem that academicians, through the awareness these metaphors have unwittingly brought, have come to view their own serious activity, like the life they have been examining, not as serious but playful, to be itself a bit of play, a game, an improvisation of hypothesized meaning.

And it is well that this should have happened in the university; or rather, it is well that it should be happening, for not all quarters of the university have been affected in this salutary way. It is well because, far from introducing a truly new view of academic life, it has served to revive a very old view whose loss we have suffered. That viewing the university as a sort of playground of ideas is an old view can easily be demonstrated by calling attention to the etymology of the word "school." Our term "school" derives from the Latin *schola* and the Greek *skholē*, which originally signified "a halt," and indicated the place or time of rest and leisure. Originally the concept of "school" connoted the way one spends one's free moments, his leisure time, his play. In Chapter 1 we mentioned a Princeton professor who defends this original meaning of humanities scholarship in a *Life* magazine article by saying: "My only message is that humanities scholarship is fun." A professor of Classics from Emory University, Douglas J. Stewart, writing in the *American Association of University Professors Bulletin* some years ago, explains carefully this old, and now rediscovered, idea of a university as a playground for life's theoretical games.

> The only reason we have a culture is that some men have retired from the world of action to play games with ideas, to set them in motion and see how and where they go. The records of their games are the stuff of the liberal arts, and somewhere some time we decided that at least some of our youth should have the lucky chance to stand apart from action and business for a term of years and enter into familiar relations with the rules of the game of thinking. We hope the liberal arts survive because we see nothing else which can produce two desirable results: first, that men so exposed generally will lead better lives of action for the experience, contributing humanely as well to the lives of others; and second, that a precious few will themselves carry on the game and contribute to our small enough stock of "reflective substitutes" for barbarous activism.[92]

The university is where the action is not; it is where the imagination is—the imagination for all action. Or so we would hope! It is the playground of ideas of play. And such play is serious business! It is the basis for whatever and wherever the action is.

But aside from being the renaissance force or midwife for a new awareness of academic life, what in fact is the significance of the contemporary fascination with ideas about games and play? Is it that in the metaphors of games and play we have the basis for the reunification of the fragmented, overspecialized disparate academic disciplines? And indeed the basis for a unified philosophy of all life? Is the implication of "play's the thing" that each man in our time should "do his own thing"? Could it be that the toy manufacturer who hit on the brand-name "Playskool" disclosed an important truth about learning theories and epistemology: that "to know" is "to play" and "to play" is "to know"? Or has the

Fisher-Price toy company hit on it when they say, "Our work is child's play"? And may it be, therefore, that Marshall McLuhan is right about education by jokes? And may it further be that we should conceive of classtime as the real recess and the classroom as the real playground? Is it that games and play are the "pause that refreshes" (the Coca-Cola philosophy) or that they are the really real life and that man should "live life, every golden moment of it" (a standpoint from an old Budweiser beer ad)?

These questions will have to remain unanswered, at least until Part III of the book. Before the *meaning* of the fascination with games and play can really be got at, there are prior questions to be dealt with, questions of how this fascination came into being in the history of human culture and in the history of the human psyche.

PART TWO

The Playground
of Being

THREE

The Origin and History of Ideas about Games and Play

*Time is a child playing, moving counters on a
game-board: the kingdom belongs to a child.*

HERACLITUS

*Truly I say to you, unless you receive the king-
dom of God as a child, you can not enter into it.*

JESUS

*I know of no other manner of dealing with great
tasks than as play. . . . In this world only the
play of artists and children comes and goes,
builds and destroys, with an eternally even
innocence and without being moralistic.*

FRIEDRICH NIETZSCHE

History and Story   In this one chance to be alive, many men have recently found themselves fascinated with the possibility of viewing life as a game, a bit of play. This we have laboriously established. Yet one question monotonously plagues our observation. From whom or from where did men get such an idea? What is the origin and history of ideas about games and play? Is the fascination really so new?

These questions are not easily put down. For still other questions plague the inquiry. Questions like: How can we answer these questions? What would a *history* of ideas about games and play be like? Can we *really* tell where certain ideas come from? Can *history* really tell? What is the nature of history? The questions stretch on monotonously and playfully in the mind of the one who wishes to search for some semblance of significance.

Perhaps one way into the vicious circle of questions, if not out of it, would be to inquire as to the history of the idea of history so that, in turn, we may better understand what a *history* of ideas about games and play might be like. Perhaps this would help; perhaps not. At least it is a way to begin.

We get our word "history" from the Latin *historia*, which is itself taken from the Greek *histōr*. This latter term literally means "knowing," being a participle of the verb *eidenai*, one of two Greek words meaning "to know." *Eidenai* (unlike the other verb meaning "to know," *gignoskō*) connotes a sort of intuitive knowledge, much the same as when we say, "Aha!" or "Oh, I see!" In fact the root of *eidenai* in the Indo-European language system is *weid*, which means "vision" as well as "knowledge," and gives us the Greek *eidos* (from whence "idea") and the Sanskrit *vēdas* (the name for a set of visionary hymns, an early Hindu Scripture, a divine revelation). Knowledge is vision. History is an idea, a vision. It is the way the historian *sees* things.

But the word-play does not end here. From fifth-century Latin forward, *historia* appears in a new form, a form that linguists call "aphesis." The new form of *historia*, shortened through the inadvertent dropping away of certain letters, is *storia* or "story." So, if history is the historian telling things the way he sees them, then his telling may as easily be called "story" as "history." History is his story; his story, history.

This suggests that the distinction between fiction and nonfiction may not be terribly important in the minds of some men. There is little basis in the beginning for a distinction between objective and subjective history. Perhaps this is what the eighteenth-century Italian historian, Giambattista Vico, meant by his phrase "poetic history,"[1] the account which is the result of the creative (*poiēsis*) and imaginative recapitulation of the past. It may well be that all historians, ancient and modern, are "poetic historians," storytellers, however much they protest *against* a bias and *for* a sort of pseudo-scientific objectivity. For is it not possible in any given history to see the clear imprint of the historian, his vision, as well as the climate of his time's opinions?[2]

So too the imprint will be clear in the following reading of the history of the evolution of ideas about games and play. If at times the account seems a bit fanciful or playful, the reader would do well to remember that, like all history, this is the author's story.

The Religious Origins—East and West   The beginning of the story of play is akin to the beginning of a recent novel by John Barth. He has on his book's opening pages a set of instructions for cutting out the page and fashioning an endless Möbius ring, a circle of the cut piece of paper made by twisting the strip once before pasting it together. If one follows the directions the result will read, "Once upon a time there was a story which began once upon a time there was a story which began once upon a time there was . . . ," and so on until one tires of reading or gets the point.[3] The origin of ideas about games and play, like Barth's self-reflexive beginning, is to be found in ancient religious ideas about origin. Theories about play begin as theories about beginning. Or, to put the matter less obliquely: both Eastern and Western religious thought contain creation stories which rely on the word "play" as a basic metaphor for understanding our world.

According to Vedantic interpretation of ancient Hindu creation hymns—to give one example—the world as we know it is a result of God's play, or what in Sanskrit is called *līla*. The world is the Holy Power played out in many names and forms (*nāmārupa*); the world, in short, *is* the play of God. Hence, what we take to be animal, vegetable, and mineral reality is actually *māyā*, the divine power of illusion. The trick of God, who is viewed as a master magician in the art of illusion, is that he "likes to play hide-and-seek." Alan Watts explains.

> But because there is nothing outside God, he has no one but himself to play with. But he gets over this difficulty by pretending that he is not himself. This is his way of hiding from himself. He pretends that he is you and I and all the people in the world, all the animals, all the plants, all the rocks, and all the stars. In this way he has strange and wonderful adventures, some of which are terrible and frightening. But these are just like bad dreams, for when he wakes up they will disappear.
>
> Now when God plays hide and pretends that he is you and I, he does it so well that it takes him a long time to remember where and how he hid himself. But that's the whole fun of it—just what he wanted to do. He doesn't want to find himself too quickly, for that would spoil the game. That is why it is so difficult for you and me to find out that we are God in disguise, pretending not to be himself. But when the game has gone on long enough, all of us will wake up, stop pretending, and remember that we are all one single Self—the God who is all that there is and who lives for ever and ever.[4]

Everything in the world is created by God. And he accomplishes the work of creation by spinning himself out in many forms. The source of such ideas about the world and its creation as a game of God is to be found both in the *Bhagavatam Purana* and in the *Vishnu Purana*, the former of which dates from the eighth century and the latter from somewhat before that time. But both are interpretations of much older ideas.

There are some who would like to think that play-theories are found only in Eastern religions. Such men feel that only in religions which do not take the world of space and time seriously can there be found doctrines of play. But the texts testify to the contrary. In fact there is as much—or as little, depending on your point of view—basis in Hebrew as in Hindu Scriptures for a play-theory of creation. The Wisdom Literature interpretation of God creating man and the world (see Proverbs 8:22–31) pictures God at play when he fashions the world and it shows man at edenic play in the pleasurable presence of God. It pictures this childlike play just as compellingly as does the Vedanta interpretation of ancient Hindu creation accounts. The only difference is that in the Hebrew story the players (*Yahweh* and *Adam*) are seen as distinct, while in the Hindu version God and Self (*Brahman* and *Ātman*) are one. But both readings set the creation scene in the context of a divine game.

The significance of the beginning of play-theory in Hebrew and Hindu interpretations of *the beginning* should be elaborated. The point seems to be that once upon a time there was an ideal situation, an arcadian perfection, a paradisiacal Eden. This was before the fall into imperfection and before the emergence of ignorant illusions about the unrealities of time and space. The pristine perfection from which we have all fully, but fragmentedly, emerged and whose bliss we therefore no longer enjoy can best be imagined as a state of original freedom unfettered by the bondage of delusion, a freedom like that of an innocent child at joyful play.

This is how ideas of play began in ancient Eastern and Western religious thought. But these lively ideas did not stand still. The ideal life of play not only was imagined before time began, but it became the goal also of after-life-time. Thus it is not surprising to discover that the metaphor of a child at play was applied, not only to accounts of Eden and Arcadia, but also to Utopia and the Day of the Coming of God's Kingdom. Doctrines of eschatology as well as doctrines of creation found the metaphor of play appropriate. The ideal state from which we were all of us banished upon the point of entrance into the life of temporal finitude is precisely the state to which we wish to return. From the gods we have come;

to their paradise of heaven we shall one day also go. Religious thought has pictured its ideal goal, before and after life, as like a child at play.

So for example, in Hebrew literature the prophet Zechariah tells of the coming of a New Jerusalem, an ideal Zion, a Day of the Lord, which Yahweh has promised for his faithful. "Thus says the Lord . . . : And the streets of the city shall be full of boys and girls playing in its streets" (Zechariah 8:3–5). The metaphor of children playing in the streets of that ideal future city is not so different from its counterpart in Christian literature. On at least two occasions the Gospels credit Jesus as comparing the Kingdom of God with children and their games and play. Chinese religion, too, is inclined—at least in its Taoist formulation—to picture the highest ideal of man in the imagery of a playful child. "He who possesses virtue in abundance / May be compared to an infant," says the *Tao Te Ching*. And of course it may be argued that the point of Hindu creation doctrines is to embody the religious ideal of playfulness. We are not to be deluded by what we take to be serious finite reality (*māyā*); it is actually and only the play of God (*līla*). Thus it is that not only before time, not only after time, but also in present time, play is the religious thing.

A striking example of the religious life of play is attributed to the sixth-century B.C.E. Ephesian philosopher Heraclitus. "Time (*aiōn*)," he is supposed to have said, "is a child playing (*pais paidzōn*), moving counters on a game board. The kingdom (*basilēiē*) belongs to the child (*paidōs*)." The saying, like all of Heraclitus' enigmas, is obscure. One is tempted to suppose that the first and second sentences of the quotation are intended as a parallelism. A child playing (*pais paidzōn*) in the first corresponds to child (*paidōs*) in the second. This leads us to believe that time (*aiōn*) in the first and kingdom (*basilēiē*) in the second are also meant to correspond. *Aiōn*, the word translated "time," connotes eternity or ultimate temporality, the whole of human existence. Thus the kingdom referred to must be some sort of ultimate kingdom, not unlike Jesus' Kingdom of God, the goal of mankind.

There are two little pieces of data that help in unraveling this ancient Heraclitean play. First, Diogenes Laërtius reports that when Heraclitus was asked to assume a position of responsibility in city government, the latter replied that it would be more virtuous for him to play knucklebones with the boys in the city's streets. And second, Nietzsche tries to show that the origin of Heraclitus' aphorism is traceable to the ancient Greek Orphic religion, whose myths include stories of their high god, Dionysos, pictured as a little child playing with toys. This divine child at play is thought to be the motivating power of human creativity; it is the symbolic representation of the transforming Dionysian spirit.

Such clues as these lead one to conclude that Heraclitus intended his meaning to suggest an ideal, a norm. Hence the saying, far from being an abstract comment about the speculative nature of temporality, contains a metaphor for morality. And this norm was originally a religious norm, having its foundation in pre-Homeric Greek mystery religion. Dionysos was the playful child. All men should emulate the divine spirit in their human spirits. Men, like their god, should master strife which is the dynamic principle in all life. And they should master it, like Dionysos, within their own playful selves.[5]

For Greek, then, as for Jew, Christian, Chinese, and Indian, the origin of ideas about play is in religion. All men, like the gods, were once like children playing. It is to the life of play that we once again aspire, now as mature adults. Our present life is virtuous, therefore, to the extent that we live life playfully, adults living the divine gracefulness of a child in the present moment.

The Philosophers' Serious Faux Pas about Seriousness   In the Genesis account, as in other religions' accounts of creation, the fall from a paradisiacal bliss of primal play is marked and marred by a new burden of labor and a bondage to a sense of life as being serious. So it is also in the history of ideas about play. Originally there was pure unequivocal play, original play-theories about the origin as play. But ambiguities were soon to creep into the metaphor. This seems to have happened initially when Greek philosophers sampled the tree of the knowledge of play versus seriousness.

Originally play was not thought of as being the opposite of seriousness. A passage from 2 Samuel (11:14) clearly demonstrates this. The sons of Abner are called on to "play" (*sahaq*), which in the scriptural context connotes a call to the quite serious activity of fighting a war. Serious activity may be viewed as play; play is serious. There is no necessary dichotomy.

One need not search long for evidence of an original unity of seriousness and nonseriousness in the concept of play. Among certain Greek biographers, for example, there is an interesting bit of evidence in the use of the word *spoudogeloios*. *Spoudogeloios* is significant because it is a word composed by joining the word for "serious" (*spoudē* also means "haste" and "zeal") with the word for "mirth-provoking" (*geloios*). Diogenes Laërtius uses the term in reference to Heraclitus.[6] Strabo attributes this term to the comic poet Menipus.[7] The finest compliment these biographers could pay to the men about whom they wrote was to call them "grave-merry" (*spoudogeloios*). It is this same high quality that must have been in the mind of Xenophon, whose ideal type was Socrates, when he recommended the life of *paidzein spoudē*, "playing serious" and "seriously playing." Seriousness and unseriousness were combined in the ideal life of some ancient Greeks.

The original absence of a distinction between play and seriousness may also be seen in the etymologies of certain terms for "play." The English word "play" is from the Anglo-Saxon *plegan*, which in its turn is from the Old High German *pflegan*. But *pflegan* gives us, not only "play," but also "plight" and "pledge." The ideas of play, plight, and pledge are semantically one. Their meanings coincide in the single concept of "duty" (German, *pflicht*). In this concept and its terminological counterparts there occurs a coincidence of the opposites of seriousness and play.

Furthermore, it is not only in the Hebrew *sahaq* that the notions of play and serious-battle come together. In Greek, too, *paidia* ("play") often connotes a counterpart, *agōn* ("strife" or "battle"). And in Sanskrit, serious erotic relationships are referred to by the term *kridati* ("play"). As we have noted earlier, *kridaratnam* literally means "the jewel of games." But in popular speech it means "sexual intercourse."[8] In English we use the expression "foreplay" in a similar manner. Such play is surely serious and nonserious at the same time!

How then in the history of ideas about games and play have we come to think of play as being the opposite of seriousness? And what are the implications of this shift in meaning? We have already hinted that the source of the shift may be found in Greek philosophy. We now ask, How so?

In response to these questions, as in response to so many other questions of Western meaning, we must look first to Plato. In the *Sixth Letter* Plato solemnly urges his followers "to live the life of philosophy," and then he adds that his advice is to be taken "in gentlemanly earnest, but with the playfulness that is the sister of solemnity."[9] In the *Laws* Plato calls the philosophical pursuit of justice "our old man's sober game of play."[10] In the *Republic* we read the somewhat surprising words: "No human thing is of serious importance."[11] Indeed, one commentator interprets the whole of the *Timaeus* as Plato consciously playing with myths from ancient Greek times. Hence Plato's philosophy may be viewed as representing the transition from a life lived under a coherent Homeric mythology to a new life lived according to the ideals of philosophy. The mythology of this new philosophy might be conceived of as a mythology of playing with mythology.[12]

Therefore, at first blush it would seem that Plato, far from being

responsible for the breakdown of the categories of play and seriousness, argues for the unity of seriousness and nonseriousness in
the concept of play. However, this turns out not to be the case
at all. Though Plato may have thought of play as the sister of
solemnity, there was a good deal of sibling rivalry in Plato's mind
and the female was not about to get the upper hand. Though the
concept of play is central in Plato's philosophizing, it is consistently
used to suggest a human activity whose ultimate goal is nonplayful
seriousness. The play of man is seen as serving the utilitarian end
of an ideal life of proper solemnity and seriousness. We have earlier
referred to such utilitarian idealism as the Coca-Cola philosophy:
man pauses to be refreshed *so that* he may better perform a life
of labor.

That Plato is the source of the Coca-Cola philosophy of play
can be seen both in the *Republic* and the *Laws*. In those works
he argues that the primary function of play is in the education
of youth. So Plato writes: "According to my view, anyone who
would be good at anything must practice the thing from his youth
upwards both in sport and earnest. . . . The soul of the child in
his play should be guided toward the love of that sort of excellence
in which when he grows up to manhood he will have to be
perfected." And though Plato writes, "now human affairs are
hardly worth considering in earnest," he goes on to add, "yet we
must be in earnest about them,—a sad necessity constrains us."[13]

This sad necessity constrains Plato to say, in the middle of a
passage on play, in the *Laws*, "every man and woman should walk
seriously." Therefore while Plato may have greatly desired that
playfulness were a possibility in the life of man, while he did in
fact say "we ought to live . . . singing and dancing," nonetheless
for Plato play served the higher end of the law and the republic,
which were themselves deemed to be philosophically serious.[14]

If Platonic idealism represents the beginning of the breakdown
of an original unity of seriousness and nonseriousness in the concept

of play, Aristotelian substantialism is responsible for the further dichotomizing of this rich dialectic. So much is this the case that it would seem never again shall the twain meet. Aristotle makes the point clearly when in his *Ethics* (X.6) he adopts the maxim of Anacharsis, "Play so that you may be serious." Aristotle elaborates this by saying that "serious things are intrinsically better than funny or amusing things, and that the activity of a man, or of some organ or faculty of his, is more serious in proportion as it possesses a higher excellence." The argument seems clear. "To make a serious business of amusement and spend laborious days upon it is the height of folly and childishness." Indeed, nothing could be more clear.

It is not that Plato and Aristotle are not in favor of the virtue of a playful attitude toward life. It is, rather, that these men subordinate the virtue of play to the higher virtue of seriousness and to the ideal of laboriously building a proper republic. In thus making play a means to another end they in fact exemplify the breakdown in an original unity. Play is now identified with non-seriousness and is therefore opposed to seriousness. It is no longer a central metaphor in which both the idea of seriousness and the idea of nonseriousness inhere. The Platonic goal of imitating an ideal and the Aristotelian ethic of realizing a potential essence mark the beginning of a sort of Puritanism in thought and ethics. Play is secondary to work; labor is primary. Or so these philosophers' *faux pas* would lead us to believe. They seduce us into viewing the world in a light which polarizes play and seriousness, good and evil, leisure and work, sacred and secular, God and man, wisdom and folly. Through the space of a few short centuries of Western thought we have come a long way from the virtue of *spoudogeloios*, indeed, from the ideal of Socrates, Plato's own master, whose wisdom and virtue consisted in the fact that he acknowledged his own ignorance. The days of such coincidence of opposite ideas were over.

The puritanical *faux pas* of Platonic and Aristotelian philosophy is serious because it has become typical of an Occidental thinking that implies that one should feel guilty every time he plays, every time he spends an enjoyable moment of leisure. The *faux pas* marks a revolution in the history of ideas which has made man feel he should constantly be working, seriously doing something serious, something useful.

The Theological Death-Knell and the Nineteen-Century Dearth   If the first false step into a dichotomizing Puritanism was taken in the idealism of Plato and the substantialism of Aristotle, the final requiem over the notion of "play" was mumbled through nineteen hundred years of Christian theological sanction of that *faux pas*. For example, St. Ambrose was fond of quoting the saying attributed to Jesus, "Woe to you who laugh, for you shall weep," and wrote that he considered that all games should be avoided. This same attitude may be seen in St. Chrysostom's sermon on a passage from Matthew: "This world is not a theatre, in which we can laugh; and we are not assembled together in order to burst into peals of laughter, but to weep for our sins. But some of you still want to say: 'I would prefer God to give me the chance to go on laughing and joking.' Is there anything more childish than thinking in this way? It is not God who gives us the chance to play, but the devil."[15]

And then there is St. Augustine who compares the life of play to vanity: "This life of ours is a comedy, imperilled as it is. For it is written: 'Naught but vanity is every man living' (Ps. 38:6)."[16] Similarly, the pietist Tollner uttered the following sentiment at a church conference: "Play of whatever sort should be forbidden in all evangelical schools, and its vanity and folly should be explained to the children with warnings of how it turns the mind away from God and eternal life, and works destruction to their immortal souls."[17] And the anonymous Puritan preacher I. G.

wrote: ". . . players assume an unlawful office to themselves of instruction and correction; and therefore it becometh sin unto them, because God never ordained them unto it, which is the reason that never any profitted in goodness but in wickedness by them."[18]

The evidence is overwhelming. Only a small portion is paraded here, but these fathers of the church are representative of orthodoxy in Christendom, which, after the manner of Plato and Aristotle, interpreted Jesus' good news about the Kingdom to mean that man had a serious obligation to imitate seriously the ideal essence laid before him by the grace of God. Indeed, what with the Greek philosophical puritanizing of the Christian gospel, the church managed to handle the concept of play about as well as Samuel Johnson's dog managed to walk on its hind feet. Johnson said about the dog: "It doesn't do it very well, but you are surprised to see it done at all."

Some of the happy surprises in the Christian tradition with regard to the concept of play should be mentioned to demonstrate that not quite the whole of Western Christendom was taken in by the ideology and metaphysics of Plato and Aristotle. Cornelius á Lapide wrote: "The son is called a child because of his proceeding everlastingly from the Father, because in the dewy freshness and spring-time beauty of his eternal youth he eternally enacts a game before his Father."[19] Gregory Nazianzus also wrote in this mode of a *theologica ludens:*

> For the Logos on high plays
> stirring the whole cosmos back and forth, as he wills,
> into shapes of every kind.[20]

Maximus Confessor wrote: "For this earthly life compared with the life to come, the true divine archetypal life, is but a children's game." And he followed it with: ". . . truly we deserve to be looked upon as a children's game played by God."[21] Clement of Alexandria spoke of the Christian life as a "divine children's game."[22] And he spoke of *mustikē paidia* ("mystical play").[23] The Venerable Bede and Bernhardt both spoke of the life of faith as a game Christians play.[24] Jerome spoke of the church as a bit of religious play.[25] And in order not to omit the usually solemn, unfestive Protestant tradition from this listing, we should mention that Luther once said that "all creatures are God's masks and mummeries."[26]

The point of these citations—which in fact nearly exhaust the possibilities of discovering the idea of the primacy of play in nineteen centuries of Western Christian culture—is that meaningful life, indeed, the religious life, may be viewed in a way different from the dominant one. Existence may be viewed *sub specie ludi*, from the point of view of play. But the quantity of evidence which can be marshaled on behalf of this minority view is pretty puny compared to the vast numbers of dry and dusty tomes which have encumbered the orthodoxast opposition to the spirit of play. Yet like Johnson's canine, it is a bit of serendipity to find even so minute a *theologica ludens* within Christendom.

Perhaps the most balanced and therefore most representative view of the nineteen-century dearth of vital and living ideas about play can be found in the writings of St. Thomas Aquinas. For in those writings there is presented a typically Western Aristotelian, and for that matter also Platonic, nod to the notion of play. It is a nod that in fact is destined to deny that which on the surface it seems to be affirming.

Aquinas seems to affirm the virtue of games and the value of the spirit of mirth in the *Summa Theologica*. At the same time he argues against the excess of either games or mirth. The argument against the excess is based upon the criterion of "the rule of reason," as he puts it. Thereby Aquinas, like Plato and Aristotle, makes the intellect primary and suggests that it would be sinful for man's will to operate out of harmony with the intellectual criterion of meaning. But to place the intellect in the role of a censor of play-activity is to make a nonplay category the criterion of judgment for play. That is, it is to raise a term other than play and nonseriousness to a place of primacy. Just *what* in fact is raised to primacy can be seen when Aquinas argues that the reason he is in favor of games is that by playing games man can rest up so that he may be better able to work. His reason for affirming the spirit of mirth is that mirth is useful for the sake of more virtuous and nonmirthful human relationships. Therefore, by operating under the axiom that man is a rational animal rather than a playing animal (*Homo ludens*), Aquinas has in fact elevated labor to a place of primacy.

Aquinas' argument is subtle. It is subtle especially when he refers to the Aristotelian virtue of *eutrapelia*, which might be translated "hanging loose," or "playing it cool." *Eutrapelia*, as Aristotle and Aquinas both argue, is the central term, the synthesis, between *bomolochos* and *agroikoi* (between "the one taking himself too seriously" and "the one who never takes anything seriously"). This is to say that *eutrapelia* is the synthesis between seriousness and nonseriousness. At first glance *eutrapelia* would seem to be the idea that we referred to earlier as *spoudogeloios*, the ideal of making play primary and central to both seriousness and nonseriousness. But on closer examination *eutrapelia* turns out to be not so primary after all, because it, like games and the spirit of mirth, is a virtue directed to the intellectualistic higher principle of rationality. It is therefore not really a primary category or a metaphor of ultimacy. Thus, Aristotelian Puritanism is here given religious sanction in the theology of Western Christendom.[27]

What we see, therefore, is that for nineteen centuries the church has continued the *faux pas* of Platonist idealism and Aristotelian substantialism by baptizing the ideals of intellect and will in the name of Father and Son. Man is thereby made to feel guilty, not only for not being able to mount the heavenly ladder to the ideal Idea, not only for not being able to realize his potential essence, but now also for his sinfulness at not being able to imitate Christian virtue by the laborious task of willing his rationality, his sanity, his *imago dei*. He cannot manage the task of building the City of God on earth as it is in heaven. It is this burden that Western man carries on his back. Stoop-shouldered from his Sisyphean labor he feels that he can only allow himself leisure and the pleasure of play when and if they contribute to more serious aims—as if play and seriousness were opposites and as if one of them therefore had to be posited as more important than the other.

The church of the Western tradition lives in that period after the Fall into a life of labor, as its Scripture in fact indicates. But that same church has not been able to anticipate the heavenly Kingdom, to which its Scriptures also refer, a Kingdom of the Spirit which, like paradise before the Fall, is pictured as a spirited life of play, where play is not laborious, as work is, but labor is playful just as games are.

The Romantic Discovery—An Eastern Wisdom Revisited   Jesus and Lao-tzu both said something to the effect that the fundamental rule of the divine game is that he who loses wins ultimately. This is certainly the case with the history of the idea of play. For though play suffered a twenty-five-century loss of place as a primary term of human meaning, the history of that failure was to become precisely the motivating factor for the ultimate victory of the idea beginning in the nineteenth century. The nineteenth century in the history of the idea of play marks the renaissance of the contemporary fascination with ideas about games and play that we have already commented on in the first two chapters.

The turning point comes when a group of philosophers decided to see what would happen to human meaning were they to make the realm of aesthetics primary. They felt that the experiment of making rationality and will primary, an experiment which had been initiated by Greek philosophers, had failed to produce unified meaning. The experiment reached the *reductio ad absurdum* following the attempt by Descartes to solve problems of human knowledge by giving ontological status to the dichotomy of thinking substance and extended substance, that is, subject and object. Not only were God and man, sacred and secular, being and becoming, play and seriousness severed, but now also the subject which wished to unite these fragmented dichotomies was itself severed from that which it would attempt to reconcile. Or as Shakespeare put it in the *Phoenix and the Turtle:*

> The heart hath reasons; reason, none,
> If what parts can so remain.

To make aesthetics primary in human meaning, as the term itself implies, is to acknowledge that man's feeling must not be anaesthetized if a human sense of coherence, harmony, and significance is to result. Rather, feeling must be seen as primary. Therefore, the attempt was made to revitalize meaning through aesthetics, that is, through the "logic" which inheres in art, in the primary human example of creation (*poiēsis*). If an artist can achieve significance in an art-work, why then, this group of men argued, may we not adopt the dynamic of the art-work as a model for the creation of meaning in human existence?

It was precisely in the attempt to identify the dynamic at work in aesthetics that the concept of play was rediscovered. The recapitulation of play as an important category of human meaning, perhaps the primary category of human meaning, appeared marginally in the philosophies of numerous nineteenth-century thinkers. The idea, however, reaches its maturity in the writings of J. C. F. SCHILLER.

Schiller identified the conundrum that had confounded Western thought for so many centuries by locating the schizophrenia of the ideas of being and becoming in two fundamental human impulses. He called these the impulse of sense and the impulse of form, "the need to discharge energy and the need to design experience."[28] He noticed that the dichotomous thinking that is based on these two impulses leads to a copy theory of reality (in Plato, *mimēsis* of the Idea; in Aristotle, *mimēsis* of the essential act). This in turn leads to a sense of fragmentation, a loss of meaning, and a resultant sense of guilt. Man cannot reconcile his need to discharge energy with his need to restrict that energy in orderly ways. Hence, this typically Western mind-set makes life difficult for the typically Western man.

It was precisely in trying to find a clue to "the difficult art of living" that Schiller discovered the concept of play. Living is difficult because serious imitation of Ideals, Law, God, Duty, Beauty, Truth, etc., is condemned to failure from the outset. A copy is never as good as the Reality. Therefore, *mimēsis* is not a category which facilitates mediation between opposites. And if we are serious about the activity of imitation the result is bound to be frustration. But if we are playful, the story is different.

Schiller found play to be a metaphor worthy of praise in the face of the difficult art of living.

> Hail to the spirit that can unite us,
> For we live really in figures.[29]

But why is the metaphor of play able to perform the magic of the *coincidentia oppositorum?* The reason is not to be found if one thinks of the use of the term "play" as merely one more clever philosophical word-game, as one further artificial conceptualization of meaning and being in the long history of the philosophical *faux pas.* The reason is rather to be found in the simple fact that play is what children do. Children—we all once knew—experience life as characterized by freedom and coherence; they experience no substantial dichotomy between the life of play and the life of seriousness. When a two-year-old boy is asked to wash his hands for supper, he embarks on a ten-minute adventure of splashing water and letting the soap slip through his hands, fingerpainting the slimy suds all over the bathroom tiles. He has no purpose in mind; he does not yet know that the point of the game is to win. He plays freely. His work is no different from his play; nor is his play different from his work. Play is the name of the unification of seriousness and nonseriousness for the child. Or as Robert Neale put it: "To have a playtime and playground with a story to tell and a game to play is to have a life of adventure that surpasses all description. . . . What happens to the child in play can happen to the adult. And when it does, paradise is present."[30] It is because the metaphor "play" carries these connotations that placing it in a position of primacy works the magic of mediation and reconciliation between schizoid categories of meaning and being.

If the category of play comes of age in the aesthetics of J. C. F. Schiller, it remained for FRIEDRICH NIETZSCHE to wed play to the modern consciousness. Just as Schiller had spotted the conundrum of Western thought in the dichotomy between the impulse of sense and the impulse of form, so Nietzsche struggled to be able to cope with the same separation, which he called by the names Dionysos and Apollo. Nietzsche, like Schiller, found the clue to the adventure of freedom and unity in a proper understanding of the primacy of play. Nietzsche wrote: "I know of no other manner of dealing with great tasks than as *play;* this, as a sign of greatness, is an essential pre-requisite. The slightest *constraint,* a *somber* mien, any hard accent in the voice—all these things are objections to a man, but how much more to his work."[31] It is therefore in Nietzsche's own playful work that our story ends.

The story had begun with Heraclitus for whom gods and men were at one through "the always living fire" whose other name is "play." Gods and men were players together, played out by the world and in relation to the world. But at the beginning of Occidental metaphysics a tendency was begun which has led Western man to conceive of Infinite Reality and finite reality, being and becoming, as separate and distinct polarities and as not at all equal. Though Plato still thought of the relation between realms to be characterized by play, nonetheless in Platonism a separation of the dichotomizing intellect and will is begun which vitally affects the way men see reality and their place in it. The play world is looked upon as being a copy of Reality. It is viewed as being secondary. Games are not to be seen as *real* life. Play is inferior. Life was thought and lived in the West as if man should unmask unreality and get at real reality—as if he were not already in the middle of it. The basis of this whole view ultimately had to be called into question. Taking oneself so seriously is too much of a burden for man to bear. Human satisfaction in the life of thought and in a thoughtful life needs a different viewpoint.

The history of the idea of play therefore is a story that once began with Heraclitus and that began anew at last with Nietzsche. The story is about a movement of an idea out of an originally religious, unified configuration, proceeding through a period of fragmentation, individuation, and breakdown, and ending with a rediscovery of an original harmony which had never been forgotten or lost in some forms of Eastern religious wisdom. The story is a story of paradise regained. It is a story, therefore, which gives man an understanding of the popularity of the idea in our own century. We are nostalgic for a lost paradise. We are attempting the remembrance of things past. We are attempting once again to catch a glimpse of "life as a children's game." These last words were penned by Maximus Confessor, about whose viewpoint Hans Urs von Balthasar has written:

Once this exalted viewpoint has been attained, all the dissonances of this world are . . . resolved in a final harmony. . . . Whoever has, even for a moment, caught sight of this vast cosmic game will thenceforward at all times know that the little life of man and all the seriousness thereof is only a vanishing figure in this dance.[32]

FOUR

The Origin and History of the Spirit of Play in Man

*For to declare it once and for all, man plays only
when he is in the full sense of the word a man,
and he is only wholly man when he is playing.
This proposition . . . will assume great and deep
significance; it will, I promise you, support the
whole fabric of aesthetic art, and the still more
difficult art of living.*   J. C. F. SCHILLER

*To become mature is to recover that sense of
seriousness which one had as a child at play.*
                              FRIEDRICH NIETZSCHE

*In the natural life of the child . . . the juncture
of work and play is fragile and doomed: soon
life will cleave in two, and work and play will
drift apart, even though they never entirely lose
contact with one another.*   WALTER ONG, S.J.

*Ontogeny Recapitulates Phylogeny, or This Is Where I Came
In*   As we move from a consideration of the history of the idea
of play in Western culture (*mythos*) to a consideration of the history
of the spirit of play in man (*bios*), a creeping suspicion strikes our
consciousness. Somewhere we have heard this story before. Taking
a clue from Joseph Campbell,[1] we might articulate the suspicion
by saying that whereas in the previous chapter we were hearing
the *mythos* of our *bios,* now we are hearing the *bios* of that *mythos.*
    Curiously, the two stories have exactly the same structure.

Nineteenth-century scholars had a name for this curious corre-spondence. They called it: ontogeny recapitulates phylogeny, the origin and history of every individual repeats the origin and history of the race. Or to give away the whole plot of this chapter at the very beginning: the story of the spirit of play in man is a replay of the story of the idea of play in Occidental consciousness. The story is—and will here be—a replay because, in the beginning, the play of a child unites his seriousness and nonseriousness, his present games and future vocation, his individual need for expres-sion and the adult demand for order (i.e., rules); thus the play of a child corresponds to the original unity of seriousness and non-seriousness in the arcadian and utopian ideals of religions and pre-Socratic philosophy. But this is not all. The transformation of play into games when the youth begins the process of socialization corresponds to the *faux pas* in the conceptualization of the play metaphor which occurred during philosophy's youth. Furthermore, adult life, which is a period of play latency, a period when the activities of children are valued as immature and/or insignificant, corresponds to the nineteen-century dearth during which moral sanction was given to a sort of conceptual Puritanism. Finally, when elder man moves into a second childhood there is a nostalgia for a lost youth, a lost sense of life and energy, of innocence and coherence; and this, of course, is very like the nineteenth- and twentieth-century quest for the rediscovery of a pristine wisdom which existed before the fall into fragmented technologism, a quest for the recovery of spiritual authenticity which existed before the fall into the long terminal religious dis-ease which ultimately led to the death of gods.[2]

The Pleasure of Primal Unity   Not only is the beginning in play, it is in "playing around." According to Sigmund Freud all children begin life as little dirty old men and women. Freud's phrase for this beginning is "polymorphous perversity." His point is this. An infant finds pleasure and significance in bodily gratification. This is of course obvious to anyone who has seen a child sucking his thumb. The pleasure which comes from infantile gratification of bodily desires has as its primary characteristic a *polymorphous* quality; that is to say, it takes many forms which from the standpoint of adult understandings of bodily pleasures must be labeled perverse. For example, an infant's pleasure has no regard for the adult barrier of species (so a child receives much uninhibited satisfaction from a puppy or kitten). The infant is insensitive, too, to disgust (so a two-year-old can receive considerable pleasure by playing with his own feces). Furthermore, the infant's pleasure transcends the incest obstacle (so bodily pleasure in a child is easily gratified by one's Mommy or Daddy). There is no regard either for the gender barrier (so pleasure can come from a member of the same sex). And finally, a child has little sensitivity to the adult "fact" that only certain organs of the body should give sensual satisfaction. While from the adult standpoint this childlike satisfaction is childish, infantile, and—if it persists in later years—perverse, nonetheless the polymorphous quality of such pleasure indicates that the distinctions which exist in the human satisfaction of adult meaning are in fact unified in the experience of the infant. Freud felt that it is "one of the most important social tasks of education" to teach the child the differentiation which will make possible adult behavior in a community environment. But of course what this implies is that the child will be educated right out of the pleasure of primal unity.[3]

Put a little differently, but still in Freudian terms, we may say that the early life of the child progresses with the following unconscious sentiments. When the child is still in the womb he feels: "I like it here. Everything is unified. I am totally at one with my world and my world is totally at one with me." This initial sentiment is changed slightly after birth when the child realizes that his immediate environment (i.e., his parents) are not a single unity, but are in fact double. Now he feels: "I still like it here very much. I feel very much at home. But the thing I like most is not one, but two." This of course is the beginning of a sense of separation. The sense of separation continues when the child notices that he likes one part of the double source of pleasure better than the other. One of his parents is at first more responsible for his sense of well-being than another. So his sentiment becomes: "I like Mommy best because she is the source of all things. I feel most at home with her." It is not long, however, until there is not only a separation from Daddy but also a separation from Mommy. It would seem the sentiment has become: "But Mommy wants me forever, so I dare not give in to her totally." As days draw on, this sentiment is altered to sound like this: "I will separate myself both from Mommy and from Daddy because their demands for me to be totally dependent on them are keeping me from figuring out who I really am. I must learn who I am. Yet I still feel somewhat attached to these figures that I now fear because together they most represent who I would like to be." In such consciousness the child slowly develops a sense of selfhood. But he does this at the risk of losing the original pleasure of primal unity.

One does not have to agree with Freud to hold this view. For in the psychology of Carl Jung, too, we discover an interpretation of growth and development which is based on an understanding of the beginning point of "wholeness, unity, non-differentiation, and the absence of oppositions."[4] In this initial stage there is operating, according to the Jungian scholar Erich Neumann, a *participation mystique,* that is, an unconscious identification which is participated in and sensed as relating all things to all other things. It is out of this originative participation, the original sense of unity, that ego-consciousness will finally emerge. According to Jung the emergence will take the form of a process of individuation in which various oppositions come into the consciousness of the personal psyche. For example, there will emerge a consciousness of male versus female forces (*anima* and *animus*) within the person. There also will be an emergent sense of good versus evil (light and shadow). A sense of rationality will contend with a sense of feeling, and a sense of intuition will contend with a sense of empirical cognition; and these will fight for the right to represent the individual consciousness in its activities of acquiring knowledge. For proper psychic growth to take place, the differentiating and individuating experience is essential. However, just as in the case of Freudian thought, it is achieved at the risk of a sense of fragmentation. The problem will become the reintegration of the total self.[5]

It has remained for the Swiss psychologist Jean Piaget to show the importance of play in the child's experience of the pleasure of primal unity. *Play*, according to Piaget, is the activity by which a child assimilates external reality to his own internal life. In this function play stands in opposition to *imitation*, that activity by which a child accommodates his own psychic life to external reality. The child begins his life in play, that is, in assimilating all external reality to his own pleasure. He then moves into an imitation stage when social reality is primary. And finally he desires to achieve a balance, an equilibrium between play and imitation.

The process can be more easily understood by noting Piaget's anatomy of growing-up. The period between birth and two years old is characterized by assimilative play. The infant plays with the sounds of his voice; he smiles at his hands and then only a moment later he examines them with great solemnity. These and so many other delightful moments are well known to all mothers and fathers who have eyes for the play of their children. What is seldom noticed is that the infant is slowly but surely transforming his artful play into the skill of assimilative make-believe. And of course he is doing this playfully, without purposive intent, without any malice aforethought. He is readying himself for the playing of games, not simply the playing of play, the former of which calls for an assimilative ability.

From two to seven years of age, Piaget has observed, there is a characteristic development from practice games, to symbolic games, to games with rules. Initially the child plays at practice games which have no symbols or rules. In this the child is like the kitten which runs after a dead leaf or a ball of yarn. As sensory and motor skills develop he becomes ready for symbolic games, like pushing a box and imagining it to be a car or train. And the more he masters symbolic games, especially those in which a totally absent object is represented, the closer he approaches the ability to play the game which has rules. Games with rules imply a sense of regulation and regularity in play in which not only are sensory-motor skills and representational intelligence necessary; reflective intelligence is prerequisite, also. It is this that later makes possible "constructional games," such as when the child hollows out a piece of wood for a boat instead of substituting the whole piece for a boat-toy. The "constructional game" is the point marking a transition from play to imitation, the transition into the ability of the individual to accommodate himself to external reality.

Hence between the ages of eight and twelve Piaget observes the decline of both symbolic play and play in general. There is an increase in work activity. This is of course important for proper development and for socialization. The only pleasures of play which remain are the games which are "made 'legitimate' by the rules of the game, through which competition is controlled by a collective discipline, with a code of honor and fair play."[6] Gone are the days of primal unity! Gone are the pleasures of play!

The Serious Faux Pas of Gaminess   When playing becomes playing-a-game socialization becomes possible and rules become necessary. The games men play make possible a liberation from childhood's ignorance; the teamwork that games require makes possible the future building of society. But not without significant sacrifice. For the rules of those games imply, not only liberation from the childish egocentricity of "mere play," but also a dutiful bondage to a sense of law and order which produces anxiety and guilt and makes childhood innocence a dim memory of an almost forgotten past.

It is the uniquely human process of symbolization that makes rules and games possible. And it is playing that makes symbolization possible. So Erik Erikson writes: ". . . child's play is the infantile form of the human ability to deal with experience by creating model situations and to master reality by experiment and planning."[7] But the mastery is achieved *symbolically*, in a realm where serious consequences are no threat because the model-play is not real reality. It is a game. This is why so many contemporary educators and industrialists recommend learning by constructing and playing simulation games. It is through games that we learn how to learn by games.[8]

George Herbert Mead explains this.[9] He explains how the child masters the symbol-making ability by moving from playing "play" to playing games. And he notes that this process is essential to proper development of social consciousness. Mead's analysis is not too different from Piaget's, but the former focuses on the origin and history of societal order whereas the later focuses on the origin and history of the individual.

Mead suggests that the ability for socialization happens in three stages. First, the child enters a "play period" in which he plays at make-believe imitations. He plays mother, teacher, fireman, policeman, and so on. But he does not yet play organized games. He is imagining himself in different social roles. And in this process he will one day discover what it means to be in a role *different from* other roles. He then knows what it means to be a self different from other selves, and therefore he can move into a second stage. The second stage is game playing and it prerequires the ability to take the attitude of all others participating in the game. "Whether the game is hide-and-seek or baseball, the demand on the player is that he discipline his self to be in a regulated relation to other selves, where all the selves have a distinct and important role to play," so argues Mead. At this stage children are fascinated by the rules of the game. They not only master sets of rules; they also make up their own rules as they go along. Rule-making enables the child to escape difficult situations that could not otherwise be handled. But rule-making and rule-mastering also gives the child more confidence in his own self-identity. And when this builds to the level of his being able and willing to risk his own identity in the presence of other persons, he is then capable of advancing to the third stage. Mead calls this third stage "the generalized other." The generalized other is a person's consciousness of the organiza-tion of all other selves into a community. Thus, in the "game stage" a ballteam is the generalized other insofar as the organization of separate team members is seen as a "team." From the experiences the child has in the game stage, he is now able to play "the game of life." But he is also on the way to viewing life as a *mere* game.

Human growth and development make possible communal cooperation, not only in the Olympic games, but also in the games of business and industry, science and art, religion and government. But this same growth and development is a first step into games of competition in which ultimately winning will become the obsessive compulsion and in which one-upmanship will become the ethical rule of thumb. When man becomes aware of this *faux pas,* he then spends the rest of his life trying to resurrect the play which characterized his childhood. He wants to play "play," not play games. It is not that he wants to regress. It is, rather, that he wants to progress, to transcend the seriousness of socialization and competition. He wants to achieve a life-style which is com-parable to the view that "actually, after all, things are not quite as real or permanent, terrible, important or logical as they seem."[10] But the harder man tries to achieve such a life-style, the more destined he seems to be to fail. There is a futility in trying seriously to transcend seriousness. The more serious one is about trying, the

more he inadvertently reinstates the seriousness which he desires
to transcend. It is like trying very hard to relax. Or like trying
not to think of blue unicorns. It happens only when you are not
trying, never when you are trying. Adult consciousness—that is,
self-consciousness or ego-centeredness or rationality or volition—
succeeds only in killing play, repressing it, forgetting it further,
or turning life into a *mere* game.

If only games were possible without the inevitable destiny of
gaminess! For there is something refreshing about the games youth
play before the nervous breakdown into seriousness, just as there
is something exhilarating about the dialogic of Socrates before the
faux pas which destined a dichotomizing philosophical consciousness. The refreshment and the exhilaration is captured in John
Ciardi's game of words: "A boy is a hurry on its way to doing
nothing."[11] The same sentiment is present in Robert Paul Smith's
nothing-is-better-than-something nostalgia:

> We spent an awful lot of time doing nothing. There was an occupation
> called "just running around." It was no game. It had no rules. It didn't
> start and it didn't stop. Maybe we were all idiots, but a good deal
> of the time we just plain ran around.
>
> What I mean, Jack, we did a lot of nothing. And let's face it, we
> still do it, all of us grownups and kids. But now, for some reason, we're
> ashamed of it. . . . There is a difference between doing nothing and
> being bored. Being bored is a judgment you make on yourself. Doing
> nothing is a state of being.
>
> Kids know about this, if you'll leave them be.[12]

The Social Sanction for Gamesmanship   Grownups of course
think they know better than kids. The anatomists of the grownups'
version of what is socially acceptable activity are the sociologists
and psychologists whom we have already referred to: Eric Berne
(*Games People Play*), Stephen Potter (*One-Upmanship*), and so on.
If their reports of the modern body politic seem sarcastic or satiric

it may be because we men spend our middle years depreciating the play of children, calling it immature, yet we ourselves at the same time proceed with our own futile games, each game having its own labored and laborious rules, with the ironic result that we never achieve human satisfaction.

Concerning this irony Simone de Beauvoir recounts the tale of Pyrrhus and Cinéas, a tale told first by Plutarch. "First we shall conquer the Greeks," said Pyrrhus. "And after that?" asked Cinéas. "Then we shall win over Africa." "And after Africa?" "We shall pass into Asia and conquer Asia Minor and Arabia." "And after that?" "We will go to the Indies." "And after the Indies?" "Ah!" replied Pyrrhus, "then I shall rest." "Then," said Cinéas, "why don't you rest now?"[13]

That we do our best to educate our young out of a sense of unity and freedom, out of a sense of wonder and joy, can be seen in the ironic book by Dr. Seuss, *The Cat in the Hat Comes Back!* Here are the opening words:

> This was no time for play.
> This was no time for fun.
> This was no time for games.
> There was work to be done.

And then the book goes on:

> Do you know where I found him?
> You know where he was?
> He was eating a cake in the tub!
> Yes he was!
> The hot water was on
> And the cold water, too.
> And I said to the cat,
> "What a bad thing to do!"
> "But I like to eat cake

In a tub," laughed the cat.
"You should try it some time,"
Laughed the cat as he sat.

. . .

And then I got mad.
This was no time for fun.
I said, "Cat! You get out!
There is work to be done.
I have no time for tricks.
I must go back and dig.
I can't have you in here.
Eating cake like a pig!
You get out of this house!
We don't want you about!"
Then I shut off the water
And let it run out.[14]

The plug has been pulled on the child's sense of unity by adulterated consciousness. And the fragmented droplets of joy have run out. This is because of a typically Western attitude toward the middle years of life. The attitude is manifested in the saying of St. Paul's: "When I was a child, I spoke like a child, I thought like a child, I reasoned like a child: when I became a man, I gave up childish ways."[15]

This attitude toward middle life is typified in Dante's *Convito* where a man's existence is idealized in terms of four stages: *adolescence* (up to age twenty-five), whose proper virtues are obedience, sweetness, sensitivity to shame, and grace of body; *manhood* (from twenty-five to forty-five), the virtues here being temperance, courage, love, and courtesy; *age* (forty-five to seventy), characterized by the ideals of prudence, justice, generosity, and affability; and finally there is *decrepitude* (after seventy), when man "returns to God" and "blesses the voyage." Dante plots these stages on life's way in the shape of an arch and identifies *the highest point* to be "somewhere between the thirtieth and the fortieth year. And," he goes on to say, "I believe that in those in perfect nature it would be in the thirty-fifth year." Since the thirty-fifth year falls in the period when temperance, courage, love, and courtesy are the central nobilities, and since Dante felt strongly (quoting Aristotle for support in his feeling) that man is basically a "civic animal," it becomes apparent that man's highest destiny, according to this typical Occidental ideal, is serious social service. Man is conceived of as wholly man when he is least like a child. Or so we may interpret this view.

In order to understand the full significance of this typically Western attitude, it is only necessary to contrast it with a statement of the Oriental ideal, an ideal whose underpinnings are a creation-faith which talks about God and the world at play and an ethos which reveres the child and the elder, this latter turning the Dantean arch topsy-turvy so that a double apex appears at both ends of life and there is a sort of sagging in the midsection. The statement we have in mind is the well-known Hindu ideal of the four phases of life (*āśramas*): *brahmacarya* (the student), whose virtue consists in practicing obedience and learning the skills and duties of his vocation; *gārhasthya* (the householder), whose role is to fulfill his duties as husband and father; *vānaprasthya* (the retiring man), whose time is ideally spent by leaving behind societal obligations and by performing the holy play of meditation; and this then leads ultimately to *sannyāsa* (the holy man), whose goal is to achieve *moksa* or "release" from and transcendence of the gaminess of all finite existence. Man becomes a child again. Adult seriousness no longer means anything to him. He is beyond all that. Quite a difference from the traditional dominant Occidental ideas and ideals![16]

In the epigraphs at the beginning of this chapter we notice that both Friedrich Nietzsche and J. C. F. Schiller lean toward the East.

For them man's full maturity is dependent upon his recovery of a sense of child's play. He must recover an Oriental *mythos* of *bios,* the original religious and pre-Socratic goal that man knew so well once upon a time. Man might well take the advice of Cinéas: "Why don't you rest now?" Or the similar advice of the cat in the hat who came back and who, laughing, ate pink cake in the bathtub: "You should try it sometime!"

When I Became a Man I Was Reborn a Little Child Again   The futility of rediscovering the play of childhood can be overcome by a sort of serendipity, by the art of finding the unexpected. A clue to such a surprise of wonder is given in a recollection of the contemporary musician John Cage: "Xenia told me once that when she was a child in Alaska, she and her friends had a club and there was only one rule: No silliness."[17] This recollection, like the play of children, is amusing. When small children play at being adult ("no silliness"), adults think it charming and delightful. Hence if adults were to play at being adult, rather than working so hard at it, would they not once again be childlike? Were such to happen we would observe that it was an accident, a happy surprise, serendipity, something achieved not by laboring at it. This is the goal at the end of life, not to win the game (we are all going to lose the game of life anyway), but simply to play and to play simply.

Charles Péguy once said, "It is innocence that is full; experience, that is empty. The child, full; man, empty. Men must learn how to unlearn." What must be unlearned is the point of view which thinks both games and work a difficult labor. What must be learned in place of such a view is the child's vision in which both games and labor are played. For as the noted physicist Robert Oppenheimer once put it: "There are children playing in the streets who could solve my top problem. They have a dimension of knowing I have lost long ago."

Play is not only a dimension of knowing but also a dimension of living and feeling and willing, in short, a way of being. It is the way that Norman O. Brown calls "dionysian consciousness."[18] Dionysian consciousness is the view of life as a festival, a dance. It is the consciousness which Nietzsche's Zarathustra has. Shakespeare said in *Lear* that "when we are born, we cry that we are come / To this great stage of fools." But it is said of Zarathustra that when he was born, instead of first crying, he laughed. The laughter of the child expresses the joy of freedom, of the sense of adventure, of delight, of pleasure. This must have been what Heraclitus had in mind when he referred to the end of life as belonging to the little child, and what Jesus meant when he said: "Truly I say to you, unless you receive the kingdom of God as a little child, you cannot enter into it." How different this spirit is from the traditional nonspirited myopia whose narrow vision is expressed in Puritanism and Victorianism, these *isms* being but the exaggeration of the dominant Western style.

Yet in the fascination with ideas about games and play there is now at last some indication that we may be moving a step beyond the traditional Western myopia. In the remaining chapters we shall examine the implications of this transformation in contemporary consciousness. We have looked at the origin and history of this new mood and mode, but we have yet to meditate on its meaning. Is modern man trying to retrieve a lost unity, to remember a forgotten paradise, to dream an impossible dream? Is he beginning to learn an old Eastern *mythos* of *bios*? "Life is a cabaret, old chum!"

PART THREE

Play's Mythology

FIVE

Play Is Religion

The trick is not to arrange a festival. The trick is to find people who can enjoy it.
FRIEDRICH NIETZSCHE

It is always good to be distinguished by something; I ask nothing better than to be pointed out as the only one in our serious age who is not serious.
SØREN KIERKEGAARD

Myth and Meaning   It was Alan Watts who once wrote: "The most profound metaphysical questions are expressed in the most common phrases of everyday life. Who do you think *you* are? Who started this? Are we going to make it? Where are we going to put it? Who's going to clean up? Where the hell d'you think you're going? Where do *I* come in? What's the time? Where am I? What's up? Which is which? Who's who? Do you mean it? Where do we get off? Are you there? . . . Is it serious?"[1]

The last of these questions has been addressed directly in the preceding chapters. In Chapter 1 we attempted to describe the modern "game point" as the contemporary tendency to call non-game events and behaviors by the name of "game" or "play." We said that the point of this is that there is a tendency in the modern world to view all life as play. In Chapter 2 we discussed a specific aspect of "the game point," that is, "the game-game," or, the academic game of formulating hypotheses and theories by extending the metaphors of game and play. In Chapter 3 the origin and history of the contemporary fascination with ideas about games and play was traced and was observed to be a very ancient and in fact originally a religious idea. In Chapter 4 we noted that the game-point tendency is further traceable, not only to ancient religious ideas, but also to the early life of every individual. This is to say that the view that life is play is based upon a largely unconscious idealizing of the life of the child, its freedom and its joy. It is to form man's future hope on a present philosophy of living life as if it were innocent play. Indeed, thus far in the book we have been addressing ourselves directly to Watt's last question only.

And yet at several points in early parts of the book we have hinted that "the game point" may represent a new and radically contemporary *mythology*. Insofar as this is the case, not only the last, but all of Watts's questions have been implicated. The *big* questions, which he has expressed in the most common phrases of everyday life, are precisely the questions whose answers are quested after and celebrated in the great mythologies of the world. If play is the root metaphor of a new mythology, then the stories in Chapters 3 and 4 are myths in a total, if as yet unconscious, mythology which speaks to all human questions, indeed, to *the* ultimate question of human meaning.

Former mythologies have been based on a single, central, "root metaphor," as Oswald Spengler called it. There is the term *logos* as the root of Greek mythology; *ma'at*, in Egyptian; *dharma*, in Indian; *tao*, in Chinese; *berith* (covenant), in Jewish; and so on. These metaphors grew quite unconsciously to the status of symbols; the symbols were spelled out into the form of stories (myths); and the stories clustered until at last whole civilizations drew their significance from a total mythology. The mythology emerged unnoticed; but the meaning was felt.

How this works can be seen in the case of the phrase "Iron Curtain." When Winston Churchill first used this phrase his purpose was to characterize a potentially dangerous political situation in a verbal figure. He wanted to name the political reality with a metaphor so that he might use the metaphor as a way of understanding and coping with the reality. As a matter of fact the aim was fulfilled. Not only was the phrase accepted as a way of thinking and speaking about a divided Germany, but it became the basis for action, too. The metaphor was literalized and not long afterward an actual wall was constructed in Berlin. The myth became not only the meaning but also the basis for the reality.[2]

Albert Camus once said, "Great ideas come into the world as gently as doves." So it is with the root metaphors and emergent mythologies of all men in all times. And so it may be also with the metaphor of play in our time. It may well be that we are becoming accustomed to viewing all things *sub specie ludi*. Play is our *mythos*. Play is a metaphor of contemporary meaning.

There are some who would try to account for our new fascination with ideas about games and play by referring to the fact of increasing amounts of leisure time in our socioeconomic mechanism.[3] But it is just as likely that the citizenry's striving for and achieving more leisure hours has been unconsciously motivated by the viewpoint (i.e., mythology) that the most desirable thing in life is play. It is not necessarily the case that the socioeconomic conditions of man determine his mythology of meaning; it is just as likely that the mythology forms the socioeconomic conditions that man desires and strives to achieve.

To put this a little differently, it would seem that it is not enough for man to be able to describe his world, his society, and his self, utilizing an object-language of nouns and adjectives. Nor is it

enough for him to be able to enact his needs and desires, express-
ing his enactments in an action-language of verbs. Something more
is needed for human satisfaction. The "more" is that man must
also be able to construct models that will serve him as guides in
his enactments and that will picture the world as he would like
to be able to describe it. It is precisely such models that are man's
myths. He creates them by the power of his imagination, utilizing
the metaphoric language of poets, prophets, seers, and revolutionaries, though often his imagining is quite unconscious. Man imag-
ines the world in which he might feel at home, and on the basis
of the imagined mythology he works to achieve the society, the
world, and the self for which he hopes. Such is the motive of
mythology.[4]

Thus in saying that play may be the root metaphor of an emergent mythology, we are implying that in America today we are
forgetting the old frontier philosophy in which the emphasis was
upon doing-centered activism. We may be witnessing a mythological revolution, turning toward a new frontier in which leisure,
meditation, and contemplation are potentially dominant. Instead
of work being our model for both work and play, play may be
the model for both our games of leisure and our games of vocation.
Play may be the mythology of a new frontier.[5]

According to one comparative mythologist the function of man's
mythology is fourfold. Joseph Campbell argues that a vitally
functioning meaning-system (1) creates in man a sense of awe at
those powers and circumstances that lie outside his control, (2)
enables man better to understand the natural world-order, (3) gives
man a framework in which society may be seen as coherent, and
(4) gives man a way to understand the intricacies of his own psyche.
A truly comprehensive meaning-system has a spiritual, a natural-
cosmic, a social, and a psychological function.[6]

If Campbell is correct about the four functions of a vital
mythology and if the fascination with ideas about games and play

represents a newly emergent mythology in our time, then it follows that the concept of play should bear the marks of these four functions. Such *is* the case. The spiritual function of the concept of play may be characterized by the word *aisthēsis*, from which we get the word "aesthetic." This dimension of the life of play may be spoken of as "nonseriousness is the highest seriousness." The natural-cosmic function of play may be characterized by the word *poiēsis*, from which we get the words "poesy" and "poetry." This dimension may be expressed as "fiction is the highest truth." The social-coherence function of play may be characterized by the word *metamorphōsis*, which may be interpreted in the case of play as "change is the highest stability." And the psychological function of play may be characterized by the word *therapeia*, from which we get the word "therapy." This function is represented in the case of play by the phrase "purposelessness is the highest purpose."

These four marks[7] and their accompanying motifs may be said to be the anatomy of the emergent mythology of play. They may be looked upon as a way of understanding the meaning of the contemporary fascination with games and play, both in everyday life and in academic matters. These dimensions of play may be thought of as a culmination of the evolution of consciousness which for the race began before Plato and Aristotle and which for each man began in childhood joy.

Aisthēsis: *Nonseriousness Is the Highest Seriousness* The fascination with the concept of play and with games is fundamentally pointing to a desire for an expansion of sense-consciousness, for the "turning-on" of all senses. Play-consciousness has a disgust for the an-aesthetic, for anesthesia, for the ascetic, for the Puritan and Victorian life-style. We only have to think of the child who delights in the experience of all senses. Or we can see the point in the etymology of the word *aisthēsis*. *Aisthēsis* comes from the Greek verb *aisthanomai,* which is the past-tense form of the verb *aisthesthai,* which means "to sense" or "to know," for the senses truly give knowledge. That the word is significant can be seen in its use by the ancient Greek translators of Hebrew Scriptures. Isaiah 49:26 reads: "Then all flesh shall know (*aisthethesomai*) that I am the Lord your Savior, and your Redeemer, the Mighty One of Jacob." Seeing is knowing; it is revelation. Seeing is believing; believing, seeing. This may have been Plato's meaning when he used the phrase *aistheseis tōn theōn,* the knowing of the gods.[8] Plato's knowledge of the gods, like that of the prophet Isaiah, is the knowing that comes from "turned-on" senses. It is the knowing of "Oh, I see!" or "Aha!" In fact, Xenophon and Euripides and other ancient Greeks used the term *aisthesis* not only to mean "to know" but also "to see" and "to hear."

Knowledge of this aesthetic sort is spiritual knowledge. It comes from a sense of awe and wonder at all things. *Aisthesis* is the dimension of knowing spoken about, for example, in a contemporary play, *The Fantasticks,* when one of the characters says:

> . . . try to see it;
> Not with your eyes, for they are wise;
> But see it with your ears:
> The cool green breathing of the leaves.
> And hear it with the inside of your hand:
> The soundless sound of shadows flicking light.
> Celebrate sensation.[9]

Celebrated, not cerebrated, sensation: the con-fusing of all senses. *Aisthesis* is body-seeing, body-knowing: seeing with the whole body, with the wholeness of the body. It is learning the joy of the expansion of consciousness, like Gulley Jimson did. Jimson, "the little creature born of joy and mirth," in Joyce Cary's novel *The Horse's Mouth* is trying to teach his mistress:

I'll show you how to look at a picture, Cokey. Don't look at it. Feel it with your eye. . . . And first you feel the shapes in the flat—the patterns, like a carpet. . . . And then you feel it in the round. . . . Not as if it were a picture of anyone. But a coloured and raised map. You feel all the rounds, the smooths, the sharp edges, the flats and the hollows, the lights and shades, the cools and warms. The colours and textures. There's hundreds of little differences all fitting in together. . . . And then you feel the bath, the chair, the towel, the carpet, the bed, the jug, the window, the fields and the woman as themselves. But not as any old jug and woman. But the jug of jugs and the woman of women. You feel jugs are like that and you never knew it before. Jugs and chairs can be very expressive. . . . It means a jug can be a door if you open it. And a word of imagination opens it for you. . . . I'm trying to teach you a big happiness.[10]

The big happiness of seeing with the imagination: *aisthēsis*. Like the seeing of the play of a child who feels with all his senses.

In these examples of the senses fully at play, exploring the dimensions of human feeling, meaning comes through the interplay of senses. The religious traditions have called the knowledge of that meaning "revelation," a new sensing of new meaning, the "Oh, I see!" and the "Aha!"

Of course there is a temptation to prostitute the spiritual dimension of play. Rather than allowing the aesthetic vision of "nonseriousness as the highest seriousness" to emerge into imagination and body-consciousness, there is often a temptation to work seriously at nonseriousness, thus raping *aisthēsis* on behalf of some overrational or overwillful attempt to take meaning by storm. This temptation emerges most often just at the point of the emerging vision of play, just at the point when one realizes the importance of dropping the gamesmanship of phony existence in favor of the pure play of authentic childlikeness. The trouble is that most persons, on dropping gamesmanship, *just work*, which is of course simply another type of gamesmanship, and not a very interesting type at that.

Or the reverse could happen. Instead of affirming the *aisthēsis* of human meaning, man might be tempted to the life of the *aesthete*, which is just another way of prostituting the spiritual dimension of play. This can be seen especially in the case of *Playboy* magazine. Robert Neale has shown the problem with the playboy philosophy. He writes:

> Nor is the playboy, despite his title, a participant in the world of play. His dalliance with women and yachts is compulsive, a neurotic attempt to deal with basic conflict. At best the playboy is *trying* to play, and the result is disguised work. He is a drudge. Pleasure may occur, but delight is entirely absent. It is significant that he cannot stop "playing," for it is the real player who reenters the work world freely and easily, with gratitude for what has happened to him, and who accepts his return with new courage and hope. That is to say, the real player is free to *stop* playing. Because the playboy cannot stop playing, he is a worker.[11]

It may well be that *Playboy* magazine has succeeded so well, not so much because of "the playboy philosophy," but simply because of the title, simply because the metaphor of play fascinates man in our time.

Yet if *Playboy* tempts some away from *aisthēsis* to the life of the *aesthete* it is nonetheless a remarkable example of the function of the concept of play in our time. In its best form, *Playboy* is a modern representation *par excellence* of the spiritual function of fascination with ideas about games and play. It is a symbol of contemporary *aisthēsis:* the turning-on of the senses, of the body-imagination. It is a symbol of the hope that *employ* may be seen as *ploy,* that nonseriousness is the highest seriousness. It is a hope for a vision of the reality of the impossibility of not being not-earnest. This hope can be spelled out in one wondrous word: joy. Such is *aisthēsis,* the primary significance of play-consciousness.

Poiēsis: *Fiction Is the Highest Truth*   *Poiēsis* is the second mark
of the meaning of the concept of play. This term has come to be
associated with the words "poetics" and "poesy" and "poetry."
Originally it was the noun formed on the simple Greek verb
meaning "to make" or "to do." Its formation implies that every
making is a doing; every doing a making. Creation is an action;
every action is a creation. Both making and doing, creating and
acting, are fabrications. They are the creative expressions of the
self. Hence, one form of the Greek verb *prospoieomai* means "to
pretend," that is, to make-believe.

Poiēsis is certainly central to the activity of play. In fact, play
is more poietic than mimetic. *Mimēsis* is imitation: the formation
of one's makings and doings so that they correspond to something
outside of oneself. But *poiēsis* is creation: the fabrication of shapes
and forms which correspond to something in one's own self. A child
plays before he is able to imitate. Play and *poiēsis* are the single
expression of the freedom of the self to make and to do anything
at all.

But why do we say that *poiēsis* is the mark of the second of
the mythological functions?—to give man a way of understanding
the natural world, the cosmos. Isn't it the case that the physical
sciences perform the function in our modern age of helping us to
understand the world about us? And aren't the hypotheses of the
physical sciences mimetic, that is, imitations of external reality?
Is it not therefore in fact the theories of the physical sciences that
perform the second of the mythological functions in the modern
world? And don't those theories accomplish this function mimet-
ically, rather than poietically, seriously, rather than playfully?

The answer must certainly be "no" if we are viewing things *sub
specie ludi*. Consider the theories of the natural sciences from the
point of view of play. Consider for example electron theory. This
is the theory that the desk on which I am now writing is mostly
immaterial space, and what is not space is really whirling atoms
composed of miniscule electrons, protons, and neutrons, held

together by electronic charges. On the face of it, this theory is fantastic. The electron theory certainly is not an imitation of the external reality upon which I am writing. It is, rather, a hypothesis which "saves the appearances" but it does not conform to the appearances.[12] The theory is a fabrication; it is the creative ordering by the mind of the scientist. It is his projection onto the external world of a sense of order. But the order is his; it exists first in his mind. His theory is *poiēsis* (creativity), not *mimēsis* (imitation). It is a bit of scientific play.

Characteristic of the world of *poiēsis* is not only that it is a world of make-believe but that it is also a world of *as if*. For example, the scientist urges me to think of my desk *as if* it were a world of whirling carbon molecules. And if I make-believe with his scientific imagination I will be better able to be at home in the external world. It is of course the same with the poet as with the scientist. Shakespeare encourages me to "willingly suspend my disbelief" so that I may better understand love in the terms of the metaphors of his sonnets. Science, poetry, and mythology are all poietic, not mimetic, if one views from the standpoint of play. Or as Martin Heidegger was to put it, quoting the poet Hölderlin: "Man dwells poetically on the earth." [13]

Thinkers have long expressed the importance of living in the world of *as if*. German philosopher Hans Vaihinger wrote a book at the beginning of this century which was entitled *The Philosophy of "As-If,"*[14] in which he argued that in order to live meaningfully in the external world we project fictions by which we order our lives. We do this, he argued, in politics, in science, in art, in religion, and so on. The fictions have no truth, but they have a truth function.

Nietzsche, too, has written, "The poets lie too much," by which he meant that the poets are metaphor-makers. A metaphor is a lie because it uses one word to speak of something else; a metaphor calls something by the wrong name intentionally, just like the scientist who calls my desk electrons.[15] Contemporary literary critic and philosopher Beda Allemann writes: "By lying deliberately, that is, by using an explicitly metaphorical language, they [the poets] are closer to truth than those who lie without being aware of it."[16] This saying is reminiscent of Picasso's statement about art being "the lie which tells the truth" and it recalls, too, the statement of Edward Albee: "A play is fiction—and fiction is fact distorted into truth." Similarly, the psychologist Carl Jung said: " 'Meaning' is something mental or spiritual. Call it a fiction if you like." And he went on to add that his psychotherapy is the giving to a patient of "the meaning that quickens," which he called "the healing fiction."[17]

The suggestion here is that in order to be truly at home in the external world, in order to understand what we like to call "reality," we have to live poetically. Or as Martin Buber put it: We have to "imagine the real." There is no other possibility. If one thinks that he imitates external reality, he is deceived, for what one is really doing is imitating his own prior projection (*poiēsis*). This is to imply that the form *poiēsis* takes, the form that the creative imagination assumes, is a pretense, a making, a doing, a *fiction* of man.

Our word "fiction" comes from the Latin *fingere*, which means "to fashion" and "to form" and "to invent." Since all our ways of thinking and seeing are our own inventions, formations, and fashionings, there is no such thing as "nonfiction." Or to put it more dramatically: "nonfiction" is a fiction, and so is "fiction" itself a fiction. Or again: in our fictions are contained our truths. Or to paraphrase Picasso and Albee: to lie is to tell the truth; to tell the truth (attempting literal *mimēsis*) is to lie. It is precisely in the acceptance of this paradox as a dimension of *poiēsis* that there is a clue to the natural-cosmic function of human meaning. This is the second important connotation of man's fascination with the concept of play.

Metamorphōsis: *Change Is the Highest Stability*   It is a short, light, and easy step from the second to the third mark of an emergent mythology of play. It is the step from *poiēsis* to *metamorphōsis:* from creation to the newness of change. It is the move from the principle that "fiction is the highest truth" to the principle that "change is the greatest stability." The move may be facilitated by referring to the strange phenomenon of the *College de 'Pataphysique* and to the remarkable book, *Love's Body,* written by Norman O. Brown.

The *College de 'Pataphysique* is a strange phenomenon in that it is a pseudo-religious cult inspired by the memory of the poet Alfred Jarry who died in 1907 after a short thirty-four-year life. The cult includes among its members men of high stature in the field of letters, men such as Jean Dubuffet, Eugene Ionesco, and others. One of the oddities of the cult is that it has its own calendar, E.P. (*ère 'pataphysique*), which reckons the years from the birth of Jarry on September 8, 1873. The *College* has an elaborate structure with professors appointed to subjects ranging from "The Dialectics of Useless Knowledge" to "Crocodilology" and "Pornosophy." Of course this is a fanciful "put-on." But it is not simply that. Jarry had defined " 'pataphysique" as "the science of imaginary solutions." Any imaginary solution is as real as any other. The only difference between one solution to a problem and another is that some perpetrators of solutions to human problems know that their structures are imaginary ones, they know that they are perpetrating a fiction, a game, and a joke, while the rest of us believe in our fictions. Or, as the statute of the *College* puts it: "All mankind consists of 'pataphysicians, but the *College de 'Pataphysique* separates those who are not ignorant of this fact from those who are."[18]

Norman O. Brown makes a similar point and in doing so helps us to see the relation between *poiēsis* and *metamorphōsis,* between the principles that "fiction is the highest truth" and that "change is the greatest stability." Let us follow his associative "logic" for a moment.

Wisdom is in wit, in fooling, most excellent fooling; in play, and not in heavy puritanical seriousness. In levity, not gravity. My yoke is easy, my burden is light.

The God of Delphi, who always spoke the truth, never gave a straight answer, in the upright Protestant way; he always spoke in riddles, in parables; ambiguities, temptations; that hearing they might hear and not understand. To teach is not to tell, is not-to-tell, like Heraclitus, the obscure. The god knew how to lie; and so did not deceive his countrymen. The real deceivers are the literalists, who say, I cannot tell a lie, or, *hypotheses non fingo*.

It is a game of hide-and-seek: "The glory of God is to conceal a thing, but the glory of the king is to find it out; as if, according to the innocent play of children, the Divine Majesty took delight to hide his works, to the end to have them found out; and as if kings could not obtain a greater honor than to be God's playfellows in that game." [Bacon]

• • •

Meaning is in the play, or interplay, of light. As in schizophrenia, all things lose their boundaries, become iridescent with many-colored significances. No things, but an iridescence, a rainbow effect. *Am farbigen Abglanz haben wir das Leben.* As indirect reflection; or refraction; broken light, or enigma.

No things, but an iridescence in the void. Meaning is a continuous creation, out of nothing and returning to nothingness. If it is not evanescent it is not alive. Everything is symbolic, is transitory; is unstable. The consolidation of meaning makes idols; established meanings have turned to stone.

Meaning is not in things but in between; in the iridescence, the interplay; in the interconnections; at the intersections, at the crossroads. Meaning is transitional as it is transitory; in the puns or bridges, the correspondence.

In the iridescence is flux, is fusion, subverting the boundaries between things; all things flow.[19]

This is the view from the playground of being where all things are playing out their own destinies. The allusion to Heraclitus is of course appropriate: *panta rhei,* "everything changes," he said. Or as the Chinese classic, the *I Ching,* puts it: "Change, that is the unchangeable."

One need only look about and observe the social order and one's own participation in it to witness the truth of the Chinese proverb. The key term for understanding the coherence of society is *metamorphōsis.* The social order is in continual metamorphosis. It is continually transforming itself, transfiguring itself, disguising itself, and revealing itself. The only thing that does not change is the appearance that all things seem to change. To try to conceive of the coherence of the social order by using a static category would be to reduce change to a nonchanging idea. Therefore the clue to understanding the coherence of the social order is to see it as not-cohering; that is the only coherent view.

Yet how does all this relate to play? Does it not seem that the player, far from achieving responsible coherence in the world of social change, is precisely the person who contributes to the lack of social coherence by his playful irresponsibility? Is not the player a person who operates under the vision of a philosophy which denies the third function of a meaningful mythology?

Robert Neale speaks to this issue perhaps more compellingly than any other writer on the subject of play.

The player is frequently accused of lacking concern for other people. Actually, it is the worker, despite his serious proclamations to the contrary, who is unconcerned. He dashes here and there in the world and keeps very busy doing good deeds for his neighbors. But the problems he perceives and works upon the world are projections of his inner problems. He is concerned about himself, and the ambivalent response to his belligerent doing of good works only dumbfounds him. The player has no inner conflict and, therefore, no need to be concerned about himself. He is free to respond to other people for their sakes and not his own. He does not abuse his fellowmen by using them as the worker necessarily does. He simply recognizes their existence. He is always surprised by them. And he is surprised most of all by the fact that they are working themselves to death. So the player does suffer, but he suffers because others work, not because he works. That is, he suffers for others rather than for himself. Now the player does not busily rush in to pick up the pieces of their fragmented lives. Rather, as a jester or clown, as a messenger from the realm of divine comedy, he demonstrates another way of life by his own behavior. The player lives as an example of what could be in the lives of his neighbors. His play is contagious, and some get a glimpse of a new world and are enticed into adventure. His suffering remains as long as there are workers in existence. But this suffering does not diminish his delight, for he remains in play, embarked on an adventure with these workers. So the true player is social and yet totally irrelevant to the world of work.[20]

To put it briefly: the player participates in metamorphosis by the very action of his way of seeing the world as play. But unlike the person who stops the flow of life or who attempts to rush the flow of life, the player does not experience change as instability. His stability is precisely in his ability to change. Novelist John Fowles has put this conclusion in aphoristic form:

Anxiety is the name we give to an unpleasant effect on us, and personal to us, of the general necessity for hazard. All anxieties are in some sense goads. They may goad the weak beyond endurance; but it is essential that humanity as a whole is goaded.

In a happy world all anxieties would be games.

An anxiety is a lack that causes pain; a game is a lack that causes pleasure.

Two different men in identical circumstances: what one may feel is an anxiety, and to the other it is a game.[21]

Therapeia: *Purposelessness Is the Highest Purpose*   We have said that the elements of meaning present in modern man's fascination with ideas about play and games are *aisthēsis, poiēsis,* and *metamorphōsis.* When these elements are at work in the life of a single individual we may say that they are contributing to that person's self-understanding; they all contribute to his personal sense of worth and meaning. And the name we may give to that total experience is *therapeia,* "therapy." The therapeutic function in the life of man is the senses turned-on to the wonder of all being (*aisthēsis*), the imagination at work projecting an order onto reality (*poiēsis*), and a life of creative action in a community of change (*metamorphōsis*). Therapy is all these things; and all these things are elements of the concept of play. Thus, we may say that the psychological function of the emergent *mythos* of play may be referred to as *therapeia.* But how the condition of *therapeia* relates to the playful life of purposelessness remains to be seen. And it may be seen through one final bit of word-play.

The Greek noun *therapeia* is based upon the verb *therapeuō,* which means "to wait upon." The condition of "waiting upon" may be understood in relation to its cognate English phrase "waiting for." The German philosopher Martin Heidegger explores the distinction between "waiting upon" and "waiting for" in a little book called *Gelassenheit.* He speaks in that book about the nature of existential meaning. He indicates that meaning is something which comes to man when man least expects it. He says that man must wait for meaning without knowing that for which he is waiting. Therefore he thinks it is more appropriate to talk about "waiting upon" meaning than it is to talk about "waiting for" meaning. For the latter would imply that the "something" for which we are waiting is already present in an idealized form. The meaning which comes to us when we "wait for" it is an old meaning; it is something that we ourselves have projected out of our past. But if we were able to wait for something without knowing what it is that we were waiting for, if we were able to "wait upon" meaning rather than to "wait for" it, then new meaning could dawn upon us. The new meaning would then not be something bound to our ego-desires and needs, but it would be something which truly participates in the wonder and awe, in the creativity and change, of all being. As Heidegger puts it: "In waiting upon meaning we leave open what we are waiting for." Such "waiting upon" makes possible ego-transcendence, ecstatically getting beyond one's own cares and anxieties which stand in the way of *therapeia*. Heidegger names the "waiting upon" with a German word that is in some ways akin to the Greek *therapeia*. His word is *gelassenheit*, which means "letting be." *Gelassenheit* has two qualities, Heidegger explains: the openness for mystery (*die Offenheit für das Geheimnis*) and the letting-be of things (*die Gelassenheit zu den Dingen*).[22]

What is implied by this is that man's noblest and most profound destiny lies in making the central purpose of his life a kind of purposelessness. For to have as one's goal a preconceived purpose is to be caught in the idealistic trap of "waiting for" an ego-projection of anxiety-laden destiny. The authentic purpose of man's therapeutic condition, therefore, would be the reverse; it would be the purposelessness which is a *letting-be* of life and meaning. This is of course what is implied when we say that *therapeia* is the internal, psychic working together of *aisthēsis*, *poiēsis*, and

metamorphōsis in the life of man. *Therapeia*, therefore, is characterized by the principle that purposelessness is man's highest
purpose. Or to put it in the words of the philosopher Eugen Fink:
"Man—as player—exists most openly to the world when he rejects
all norms and when he is bound by boundlessness."[23]

Play Is Religion   The business of mythology is serious business.
It is the affair of human meaning. Joseph Campbell once wrote:

> Clearly, mythology is no toy for children. Nor is it a matter of
> archaic, merely scholarly concern, of no moment to modern men of
> action. For its symbols (whether in the tangible form of images or in
> the abstract form of ideas) touch and release the deepest centers of
> motivation, moving literate and illiterate alike, moving mobs, moving
> civilizations. There is a real danger, therefore, in the incongruity of
> focus that has brought the latest findings of technological research into
> the foreground of modern life, joining the world in a single community,
> while leaving the anthropological and psychological discoveries from
> which a commensurable moral system might have been developed in
> the learned publications where they first appeared. For surely it is
> folly to preach to children who will be riding rockets to the moon
> a morality and sociology based on concepts of the Good Society and
> of man's place in nature that were coined before the harnessing of
> the horse! And the world is now far too small, and men's stake in sanity
> too great, for any more of those old games of Chosen Folk (whether
> of Jehovah, Allah, Wotan, Manu, or the Devil) by which tribesmen
> were sustained against their enemies in the days when the serpent
> still could talk.[24]

It is serious business; it is the affair of meaning. And in our time
the meaning, along with the former mythologies, seems to have
collapsed. We are accustomed to viewing ancient and traditional
meaning-mythologies as playthings, toys, or games. We view
mythology playfully. We view the world of the ancient myth-
makers as a world of "as if" and "make-believe." But our way of

viewing mythologies of meaning gives us away. It tells the tale of our own mythology of viewing former mythologies. And the tale says that we view playfully; our view is play. Play is our mythology.

Marshall McLuhan, a contemporary anatomist of human myths of meaning, has put this same point just a little differently. He views man's literal games as an extension of his meaning, of his serious everyday life. He writes that "the games of a people reveal a great deal about them. Games are a sort of artificial paradise like Disneyland, or some Utopian vision by which we interpret and complete the meaning of our daily lives. In games we devise means of nonspecialized participation in the larger drama of our time." [25] It follows from McLuhan's view not only that our games are extensions of our nongame life, but also that our nongame life's meaning is an extension of the games we play. Man is a player. Play is the root metaphor of his meaning.

We might say that the articles of the creed of contemporary meaning go something like this:

Our day:	playday
Our time:	playtime or recess
Our people:	playboys and playmates
Our world:	playground or playroom
Our society:	games

This unconsciously operating play-mythology corresponds to the requirements of a truly modern meaning-system as outlined by Northrop Frye in a book called *The Modern Century*.[26] In that book Frye comments on the failure of former mythologies in our time. He indicates that the reason they have failed has to do with the fact that they were "closed mythologies." Frye says that a truly contemporary meaning-system will be characterized by its "openness." Thus it will not be as well unified as earlier mythologies; it will have neither a canon of scripture nor an elite class of insiders.

A modern meaning-system will be, Frye believes, aesthetically based, that is, directly related to the creative arts. And it will compel men through the hope and possibility of a life governed openly by the poesy of make-believe rather than by the creedalism of belief. The only difference between our own analysis and Frye's is that he does not use the term "play." But the meaning is the same. To put it once more in the terms that we have been using: insofar as *aisthēsis, poiēsis, metamorphōsis,* and *therapeia* are truly the elements which inform man's hope for meaning, to that extent the mythos of play is emerging as a vital root-metaphor of contemporary human meaning.

But, if this be so, another conclusion is warranted, also. The famous scholar of religions Joachim Wach once said that "the primary theoretical expression of the religious experience is myth."[27] Thus, to the extent that the meaning-system whose root metaphor is play is vital in our time, to that extent play is not only man's myth but also his religion. This is to say: the four elements of the play mythos are that which concerns man ultimately; they are that which man quests for and celebrates in moments of festivity.

But to refer to play as the religion behind man's everyday existence is to imply a radical reformation in the history of religious consciousness. It is to imply that there has been a subtle transformation in the locus of religious meaning. Whereas previously man found meaning in social contexts, now he finds it individualistically. This is reflected in man's concern and anxiety, his negative feelings about gamesmanship. It is reflected also in man's desire for play, with its accompanying four functions. In the life of an individual, the ability to play *games* is achieved when man is capable of socialization for the first time. Play itself is an individual matter, but games are a social affair. Now if what is desired is to overcome gamesmanship and to discover, or rediscover, the authentic play whose key categories are *aisthēsis, poiēsis, metamorphōsis,* and *therapeia*, there is represented an intuition about the locus of meaning not being in the tribe, the nation, the local group, the church, or the synagogue, but, rather, being located in the individual.

Such an intuition about the meaning of the play mythology corresponds to some comments about modern mythology written at the end of *The Hero with a Thousand Faces*. In this book Joseph Campbell notes that "today all of these [society's traditional] mysteries have lost their force; their symbols no longer interest our psyche. . . . Not the animal world, not the plant world, not the miracle of the spheres, but man himself is now the crucial mystery." Because of the failure of social supporting meaning-systems, the individual is thrown back upon his own resources; he is plunged deeply into his own inwardness. He is exiled from social duty and the popular cultic games; he sees through them; he finds them phony and empty, vacuous rituals of life and belief. Hence he begins the quest for meaning on his own. "He is driven to his own profundity and breaks through, at last, to unfathomable realizations. No man can return from such exercises and take very seriously himself as Mr. So-and-so of Such-and-such a township, U.S.A.—Society and duties drop away." The modern creative hero is not guided by society, but modern society will be guided by the creative individuals of our time. For it is the task of man today "to learn to recognize the lineaments of God in all of the wonderful modulations of the face of man."[28] It will take much freedom, much humor, much love, much play (*aisthēsis, poiēsis, meta-morphōsis, therapeia*) to realize such true humanness.

But even if it were possible, which of course it *is* naturally for the child and may one day also be for all men, the gain is not without loss. For if our religion is play, if it therefore be centered in individuals rather than in collectivities, what becomes of the traditional religions, whose locus of meaning was the group? What for example becomes of the institution of the church? This of course was the problem presented dramatically by the "death-of-God" theologies of several years ago. And it is the problem we will address in the final chapter. If our real, however unconscious, "religion" is play, what then becomes of the traditional religion to which we still may give conscious, if only lip-serving, allegiance?

SIX

Religion Is Play

Theology is the art of befuddling oneself methodically.   JULES MICHELET

A theologically informed investigation of man as imaginer, player, and hoper (homo ludens et sperans) *instead of man as sinner, or even as creature, might yield some beneficial results.*
HARVEY COX

Religion Is Play   The problem of what becomes of traditional religion when one lives a life of play is not so difficult as it may seem. For if our real religion is a mythology of play, if we are in fact coming to view all things *sub specie ludi,* then traditional religion, like everything else under the sun, is seen as play. The only real problem is what to do with our very old, and very serious (i.e., orthodox), theologies which do not see things this way. They are out of date. Perhaps that is why theology befuddles us. And perhaps that is why one contemporary theologian, Harvey Cox, thinks a theology of play, to match our contemporary religious consciousness of play, might help.[1] What we need is a *theologia ludens,* as Jesuit Hugo Rahner has called it.[2]

A *theologia ludens*—the interpretation of traditional religion as play—would view God as a player, man as a player, the church as the community of play, salvation (both now and in the life to come) as play, and morality as *eutrapelia*.[3] This is precisely what Rahner has outlined in his brilliant little book, *Man at Play*.[4] It is what Romano Guardini was attempting when he wrote, some years ago, that worship is "a kind of holy play in which the soul, with utter abandonment, learns how to waste time for the sake of God."[5] It is what several Church Fathers knew[6] and what St. Thomas was attempting when he wrote:

> The contemplation of wisdom is rightly compared with games, for two things are to be found in games. The first is that games give pleasure and the contemplation of wisdom gives the very greatest pleasure, according to what Wisdom says of itself in Ecclesiasticus, "My spirit is sweet above honey." The second is that the movements in games are not contrived to serve another end, but are pursued for their own sake. It is the same with the delights of wisdom. . . . Hence divine Wisdom compares its delight to games, "I was with him forming all things and was delighted every day, playing before him at all times: playing in the world."[7]

And it is what Meister Eckhart achieved:

> This play was played eternally before all natures. As it is written in the Book of Wisdom, "Prior to creatures, in the eternal now, I have played before the Father in an eternal stillness." The Son has eternally been playing before the Father as the Father has before the Son. The playing of the twain is the Holy Ghost in whom they both disport themselves and he disports himself in both. Sport and players are the same. Their nature proceeding in itself. "God is a fountain flowing into itself," as St. Dionysius says.[8]

The time is ripe for a *theologia ludens*. We need and desire a new and radical theology whose basic nature is *aisthēsis*, and whose characteristics are *poiēsis, metamorphōsis,* and *therapeia.*[9] This is the religious dimension of the point about "play" in our time. It is the religious implication of our contemporary fascination with ideas about games and play.

It has not been too many years ago that, during the annual convention of the American Academy of Religion, three theologians wandered into the cocktail lounge of Chicago's Conrad Hilton Hotel. They were served by a scantily clad waitress with whom, after several drinks, they had the following conversation.

"What do you think we do for a living?"

"I'd guess you are cartoonists," she shot back, grinning.

"We are theologians," they one-upped.

But she reployed, "That's something to do with divinities, isn't it?"

To which they had to confess her original accuracy: "Yes. Cartoonists of divinities. Caricaturists of God!"

That is the way with theology. Too much of it has been a caricature. Too little of theology has been articulated in a mode appropriate to its religious subject matter. It has therefore been idolatrous. Its message of grace and salvation has too seldom been manifest in its medium. Rather, the message of its befuddling medium has been, not gracefulness but tedium. It is therefore not enough for a *theologia ludens* to be a theology about play, interpreting traditional doctrines of the faith *sub specie ludi.* At least this is not enough if a *theologia ludens* is to avoid being inadvertently a ludicrous theology. Something more is needed. It must not only be *about* play; it must also be a theology *of* play, *by* play, and *for* play; it must wittingly incarnate its content. The ultimate concern of a play theology, therefore, is not so much the articulation and understanding of the faith of the church (a traditional definition of theology) as it is to articulate and understand the articulation and the understanding. The message is freedom; theology's medium must be free. The message is grace; theology's medium must be graceful. The message is spirit; theology's medium must be spirited. Perhaps this is why G. K. Chesterton is remembered as holding the opinion that the religion of the future will be based on a highly developed and highly subtle form of humor.[10]

Aphorism: The Language of a Theology of Play   The concern with theological method is not a new concern. It is as old as the misunderstanding surrounding Jesus' use of a medium which would properly embody the message of which he himself was the true embodiment. "All this Jesus said to the crowds in parables; indeed he said nothing to them without a parable."[11] "Then the disciples came and said to him, 'Why do you speak to them in parables?' And he answered them, '. . . I speak to them in parables, because seeing they do not see, and hearing they do not hear, nor do they understand.'"[12] St. Paul was getting at the same concern when he wrote: "And we impart this in words not taught by human wisdom but taught by the Spirit, interpreting spiritual truths in spiritual language."[13]

The problem of a theological method appropriate to the religious message is a problem of language. It is a problem whose risk is idolatry, the prostitution of the message with an inapt medium. It is a problem which has more and more confounded contemporary theologians.[14] And it is a problem which is raised especially in the case of a play theology. For the language of an authentic theology of play, by play, and for play must be not only aesthetic, poietic, metaphoric, and therapeutic in form and function; it must also be precisely of play, by play, and for play.

It is not that the language of a theology of play must be nonserious. We have already seen that seriousness is not the opposite of play. It must, rather, transcend seriousness, just as play is a category which transcends and unites seriousness and nonseriousness. Any form of language (such as *mere* discursive and literal prose) which is caught in the serious versus nonserious, the literal versus symbolic, dichotomy will not do. The language-form of a theology of play is not a word of dichotomous and schizophrenic nay-saying in opposition to other words. It is beyond such noisy chatter which opposes it. It is not the language of noisy gongs and clanging cymbals; it is, rather, the language of love, of yea-saying. It is a language-form which is inclusive, not exclusive. It "lets be" (*Gelassenheit*).

The language-form of a theology of play, like the language-form of a joke and like life itself, is pregnant, full of puns and possibilities. It is open. It lets all possibilities, hopes, dreams, and meanings be, so that they may become what they in fact are. Like the *double-entendre* of a joke, the language of play theology is nonperspectival, nonopinionated, nonorthodox. Being nonperspectival, it is a veiw from the horizon. It toys and games with partial provincialisms in order to transcend them in play. It is encompassing. It is horizontal in that it is holistic. But what is it?

There are many *its*. Perhaps even all language-forms participate in this open-nature at their imagistic roots. But at least one form of horizontal thinking and speaking that can be identified is aphorism: *apo* = from; *horidzōn* = horizon. An aphorism is a definition which is open-ended. Its end or goal or purpose is open. Its purpose is purposelessness. Its end is openness. It achieves its function because of its fundamental ambiguity and, thus, it is like a joke.

A joke is an aphorism with a punch. And an aphorism is a joke whose punch is hidden. Like a dream, its therapy is in a transforming revelation which is ambiguous enough not to be resisted. Its function is to reveal the hiddenness of the hidden while retaining the essentially esoteric quality of man's mysterious nature and destiny.

The form of an aphorism may be likened to that of a parable. We were all taught in basic grammar and rhetoric class that every proper paragraph should be composed of two things: a single topic sentence, and illustrations which make the topic sentence compelling. This is what makes for a sound argument and a compelling paragraph, or so we were instructed. Well, be such instructions as they inevitably must be, a parable is a paragraph without a topic sentence (or we might have said, a fable without a moral or an extended metaphor without a conclusion), and an aphorism, conversely, is a topic sentence without the paragraphic logic or illustration attached.

However improper sophomoric rhetoricians may think such language-forms, there has been a long and not-unsophisticated tradition of aphorists, not to mention parabolists. It is by aphorism that aesthetic sensibility has been able to inform philosophy, as in the writings of Heraclitus,[15] Montaigne,[16] Lichtenberg,[17] and Wittgenstein.[18] These names represent a tradition in thought different from the rationalizing, objectifying one from Plato through Hegel, the major tradition of the *faux pas* of play versus seriousness. They are distinguished and characterized by the linguistic form they employed: aphorism. And in its aphoristic form philosophy is dynamic and nonobjectifying.

Philosophic aphorisms, according to Lichtenberg, "give an insight and divulge something of the way the insight has been attained." Hence, "an aphorism is true when it has fixed the impression of a genuine experience." "The aphorist, bending over the stream of language, found in it his own image: but the hump did not show, and his face, its traces of suffering softened by the ripples of water, was framed in trees and blue sky."[19] The philosopher as aphorist is a philosopher of play at play. He is a practitioner of philosophy informed by self-awareness (*therapeia*). "*Que scais-je?*" Montaigne asked. "You could not discover the limits of soul, even if you traveled every road to do so; such is the depth of its meaning," wrote Heraclitus; and then he added, "The hidden harmony is better than the obvious."[20] And Wittgenstein:

We want to say: "When we mean something, it's like going up to someone, it's not having a dead picture (of any kind)." We go up to the thing we mean.

"When one means something, it is oneself meaning"; so one is oneself in motion. One is rushing ahead and so cannot also observe oneself rushing ahead. Indeed not.

Yes: Meaning is like going up to someone.[21]

Nietzsche's name should be mentioned, too, as a philosopher who participates in the aphoristic tradition. Mention of his name, along with that of Heraclitus, is especially significant. These men were named earlier as exemplars of a philosophy whose key category is play. So it is apt to find them a part of the aphoristic tradition, too.

If theology wants a philosophical method or a philosophical dialogue partner, it would do well to consider the aphorisms of these play philosophers, not for their philosophical substance, but for their philosophical style; not for their message, but for their media. The methodology of the aphoristic tradition in philosophy should be a clue to a theological method appropriate to the theological message. It should be a clue for a theology of play.

Of course this advice is not new. Some theologians have considered and consented to an aphoristic mode. Their work becomes the paradigm for a theology of play. One thinks immediately of the book by Nicholas of Cusa (Cusanus) written in 1463 just before his death, which was titled *De Ludo Globi* ("The Ball Game").[22] Cusanus meant his aphoristic dialogue as a metaphor of how man may attain spirituality. He may do it in the same way that he plays "the ball game" which Cusanus invented. Karl Jaspers explains the game:

It is played with a wooden ball with a spherical hollow off center. When the ball is bowled, it does not, since one side is heavier than the other, roll in a straight line, but takes a spiral path. The players toss the ball over a surface divided into ten concentric circles. At the center is the king—Christ. The winner is the player whose ball has touched the greatest number of circles and comes closest to the center.[23]

By playing this game the player participates in the mystery of the doctrine of God, which the game symbolizes.

But Cusanus is not alone in such theologizing. There are the *Pensées* of Pascal, the *Confessions* of St. Augustine, *In Praise of Folly* by Erasmus, and of course Kierkegaard, who wrote, "the highest earnestness of the religious life is recognizable by the jest."[24] In the listing of theologians whose life- and writing-style prefigured a contemporary theology of play, Clement of Alexandria should perhaps head the role. Clement's most mature work was a poetic and aphoristic *Rag Bag* (*Stromata*) whose purpose, as he himself put it, was "to pass on hidden things of truth in a way showing reverence to God."[25] He insisted on the aphoristic, patchwork form of theology because "all things that shine through a veil show the truth grander and more imposing; as fruits shining through water, and figures through veils, which give added reflections to them."[26]

Make-Believe: The Faith behind a Theology of Play   If aphorism is a *theological* form of the religious play that transcends the games of this world, then what *religious* form does play take? The traditional answer to this question is, of course, "faith." But as long as we continue to think of faith as belief, and as long as we continue to think of faith's opposite as nonbelief, we will not have transcended this world's opinions and games. *Sub specie ludi,* from the point of view of play, from the horizonal aphoristic viewpoint, faith transcends belief and nonbelief. Faith is make-believe.

Robert Neale has argued the case for make-believe as compellingly as any other. He points out that there are three possible responses to sacred dimensions of life: the magical, the profane, and the religious. The first of these, the magical, is the response which attempts to control those dimensions of life that lie beyond one's control. The profane response is the denial of those aspects of life which are beyond one. Both the magical and the profane responses to the sacredness of life are work-serious responses. They both wish to manipulate life and meaning by a laborious act of reason or will. Only the authentically religious response is characterized by the ability to "let be," as Heidegger puts it; the ability to "accept the fact of acceptance," as Tillich calls it; the ability to be a play-filled "adventurer with the playtime and playground of the play world," as Neale says.[27]

Neale notes that the magical response has as its central quality "belief." The profane response is of course recognizable as "non-belief." The truly religious response, characterized by the elements of play, should be called, Neale feels, by the name "make-believe." For in the life of authentic faith

> questions of truth and falsity remain irrelevant. Unless belief and disbelief are transcended, the life of adventure in the partial play of the immature, or in the full play of the religious adult, does not occur. When an individual becomes concerned about the validity of a story [like the Christian gospel], he has entered into the realm of the profane.

Neale goes on:

> The magical mingling of the sacred and the profane issues in the promotion of belief. Belief is the acknowledgement of the sacred for the sake of the profane, a work reaction to the manifestation of new energy and new design. One always believes "because." The mother believes in play because it will remove her child's restlessness. The adult believes in the sacred because he will receive wealth or health. The statement, "I believe," is always incomplete. So the primitive magician affirms, "If I pronounce the sacred words over the sacred symbol, I will catch fish," and the modern magician states, "If I say my prayers, I will receive strength for tomorrow." Consequently, the

call to believe is usually accompanied by promise of benefit or threat of harm, and these promises refer to the struggles of profane living. Even such seemingly benign statements as, "I believe because of what God has done for me," or "I believe because I have received meaning for my life," represent the attempt to make the sacred useful for profane life. The magician is a pragmatist who believes the sacred story is true because it works. Thus, belief is the result of an inappropriate work response to what offers the potentiality for play. The sacred is purposeless, and the attempt to use it is antireligious.[28]

The case for faith as make-believe is supported not only by the psychological arguments which Neale calls upon, but also by the language of the New Testament and the history of Christian thought. The New Testament word that is ordinarily translated by the English verb "to believe" is a Greek verb (*pisteuō*) based on the noun meaning "faith" (*pistis*). What is fascinating about the Greek verb is that it is never followed by the preposition "in," as our translations would lead us to believe. It is always used with the preposition meaning "into" (*eis*). Hence, where we read "believe in," the original text literally means "faithing into."

The problem of mistaking faith for belief arises because Latin, French, English, and other Western languages do not have a verb based on the noun meaning faith. Latin has *fides* for "faith," but the verb meaning "to believe" is *credere*. French has *foi* and *croire*. And in English we do not say, "I faith," but rather, we say, "I believe." But this implies "I believe *in* something," a very different implication from "faithing into."

This misunderstanding between faith and belief was a problem that was not ignored by the thinkers of the church. When the early theologians talked about faith as belief (*fides* as *assensus*, faith as assent to something taken to be true) they anxiously added that faith is not enough in the life of man. It must be complemented by charity and hope.

The reformation church, too, and especially Martin Luther, preferred the word *fiducia* to the word *fides*, because *fiducia* can never be confused with belief *in* something taken to be true. It, rather, means "trust" and "confidence." A man can have trust and confidence without solving the problem of whether or not the object of his trust and confidence is true or false. So, in this sense, a man may have trust and confidence in his wife without having a compulsion to have a private detective follow her to make sure she is true. He trusts her and has confidence in her. This does not mean that he believes she is true. It means something far more important than that. It means he makes-believe she is true. It would be an insult to her and to his faith in her if he were to question the truth of her every emotion, act, and thought. It is the same in religion. Faith is not mental assent or emotional assent, either, whose object is a belief in some supernatural or historical datum which dogmatically and zealously insists on its truth.

But, then, what is faith? Consider these two stories.

The noted anthropologist Leo Frobenius tells about a colleague of his at the university:

> A professor is writing at his desk and his four-year-old little daughter is running about the room. She has nothing to do and is disturbing him. So he gives her three burnt matches, saying, "Here, Play!" and, sitting on the rug, she begins to play with the matches, Hansel, Gretel, and the witch. A considerable time elapses, during which the professor concentrates upon his task, undisturbed. But then, suddenly, the child shrieks in terror. The father jumps. "What is it? What has happened?" The little girl comes running to him, showing every sign of great fright. "Daddy, Daddy," she cries, "take the witch away! I can't touch the witch any more!"[29]

The second story is very much like the first. A father was awakened in the middle of the night by the screams of his three-year-old daughter. He rushed to her bedroom and asked what was the matter. Sobbing, she pointed in the direction of her dresser and whispered, "A monster! A monster!" The father looked. The street-light was reflected through trees and windows in such a fashion as to transform the dresser-drawer knobs and mirror into a fearsome sight indeed. So the father simply flicked on the bedroom light, with the reassuring words, "See, Honey, no monster, just your dresser. OK?" She assented. It was OK. The father kissed his daughter good-night and left the room, flicking off the light as he went. No sooner had the light gone out, however, than the screams returned. The monster was back!

The point is simple, as simple as the wisdom of a playful child. Faith is being gripped by a story, by a vision, by a ritual (game). It is being seized, being gripped by a pattern of meaning, a pattern of meaning that affects one's life-pattern, that becomes a paradigm for the way one sees the world. It is not belief. These kids do not believe in this business, at least they do not believe in thoughtful reflection when the mind's light is on. But neither does the efficacy and the meaning-function depend upon their believing *in* the truth of something. Belief is beside the point. Faith is not belief. It is not intellectual assent. It is not some ritual played *so that* something will happen. Faith is being turned on by an incredible vision. It is make-believe. Questions of truth and falsity remain irrelevant. Belief and disbelief are transcended in authentic faith.

Faith is make-believe. It is playing as if it were true. It is not that the religious story is not true. It is simply that questions of truth are irrelevant while in the midst of make-believe, while in the midst of faith.[30]

Make-believe is play-faith. It is the faith that Jesus spoke of: "Unless you have faith like that of this little child . . . ." It is the faith we may hold in the midst of doubt. Or rather, it is the faith that holds us in the midst of our doubt. It is the faith which says: "I believe, help my unbelief!"[31]

Perhaps one more story is appropriate. The setting is the backyard of a suburb of New York City. A sophisticated corporation executive is speaking.

"We're going to do it up right this Christmas. We're going all out. We're going to spend a lot on gifts for our kids. More than ever before. You know why? Because this is the last year our kids will believe in Santa Claus. And that makes me kind of sad. You know, I think I get more out of it than the kids."

Of course! When we are kids we believe naïvely. We play. Then we begin to grow up. We begin to have doubts. We learn the rules of the games. Until at last we come to full-fledged disbelief. Trapped by gamesmanship. But just at that point a funny thing happens. We have kids of our own. And while they are in the same stage we were in once upon a time, we play the game with them. We make believe. And it is true; we get more out of it than they do. Why? Because belief that is not matured by doubt is not true faith. Naïve play is no better for the mature man than his ironic gamesmanship. We cannot go back. But we hope to go on. Faith that does not go beyond naïve belief *and* rebellious disbelief is not true faith. Yes, Virginia, as the saying goes, there is a Santa Claus because there is a Santa Claus story. A fairy tale; a gospel. And the gospel is good news (good *spiel;* good play). It grabs me. It turns me on. It makes a swinging Christmas possible. Belief and disbelief are beside the point. Make-believe is the game point in religious life. Or, as Joseph Campbell put it:

From the position of secular man (Homo sapiens), that is to say, we are to enter the play sphere of the festival, acquiescing in a game of belief, where fun, joy, and rapture rule in ascending series. The laws of life in time and space—economics, politics, and even morality —will thereupon dissolve. Whereafter, re-created by that return to paradise before the Fall, before the knowledge of good and evil, right and wrong, true and false, belief and disbelief, we are to carry the point of view and spirit of man the player (Homo ludens) back into life; as in the play of children, where, undaunted by the banal actualities of life's meager possibilities, the spontaneous impulse of the spirit to identify itself with something other than itself for the sheer delight of play, transubstantiates the world—in which, actually, after all, things are not quite as real or permanent, terrible, important, or logical as they seem.[32]

EPILOGUE

Beyond the Rules of the Religious Game toward a Theology of Play, by Play, and for Play

True eloquence makes light of eloquence, true morality makes light of morality; that is to say, the morality of the judgment, which has no rules, makes light of the morality of the intellect. For it is to judgment that perception belongs, as science belongs to intellect. Intuition is the part of judgment, mathematics of intellect. To make light of philosophy is to be a true philosopher.   BLAISE PASCAL

Books should be about themselves. They should manifest their content in a medium which reflects the content. They should manifest a reflexivity of internality, being internally consistent in subject matter and mode of expression.

Perhaps every book *is* about itself, whether the author intends it that way or not. Perhaps its manner of expression does in fact reveal what is ultimately concerning the author. But if every book is about itself, it is this most often unwittingly.

If a book purports to witness to life lived *sub specie ludi*, perhaps then there should not be a serious word in the whole book. Some authors have hoped that readers would not take them seriously. St. Thomas Aquinas called his writing "so much straw." Plato, commenting on Socrates' not-publishing and perishing, said that serious teachers do not write books. And remember Jesus' publication record!

The corollary to the fact that serious teachers do not write may be that serious writings do not teach. If this be so, I seriously hope there is not one serious sentence in the whole of this book. Including this last one.

Marshall McLuhan was quoted in the epigraph to the first chapter as saying that "a perceptive or incisive joke can be more meaningful than platitudes lying between two covers." The danger with a book like this one is that someone might take it seriously. Or that the author might take the preceding sentence seriously.

The difficulty here is like the difficulty of the lover. When he is most serious he must say to his mistress: "I wouldn't dare treat you seriously. We are playing around. Especially I wouldn't dare treat you seriously if I feel seriously about you—for fear of destroying our relationship with intensity and tenseness. Rather than treat you seriously, I will play with you—toy with you. You are my kitten. We will have a ball! Of string! Stringing each other on! Like this conversation!"

The persons with whom one has all the time to be serious, the ones with whom one cannot "play around," the ones that one cannot "toy with" and "put on"—such persons are the ones with whom the relationship is tense without being at the same time intense.

> Taking fun
>   as simply fun
> and earnestness
>   in earnest
> shows how thoroughly
>   thou none
> of the two
>   discernest.[1]

Someone said that fools are the wisest persons in the world and that the wise are mere fools. This is like saying that clowns in order to be true clowns must at the same time be truly sad. What it all comes to is that sad and happy, foolish and wise, are dialectics, not dichotomies. You can't have one without the other. So it may also be with play.

There is indeed not one serious word in this whole book. But then there is not one nonserious word here either. That is the point about play: the game point.

What's the name of the game? That's it. The name of the game is: What's the name of the game? It is the game we all play. And often we play it quite seriously, desperately in fact, trying to identify the other person's game. In fact we play so seriously that we forget to play. That is, we forget that we are hard at play calling our play not-playing.

Of all the dances men dance in this crazy choreography of life the most insane and at the same time the cleverest one is the dance men dance when they claim to be not-dancing.

Just as there is no such thing as not-dancing (the man who thinks and feels he is not dancing is simply doing an intricate piece of side-stepping), so also the dancer who says that another person is not dancing is himself doing a strange dance. He is dancing the not-dance, because he, at that moment, does not have dancing eyes to see the not-dance dance of another as itself an intricate dance.

Some will say: "But there comes a time when things get serious." On the other hand, there is a saying in the vernacular: "You can't be serious!" The common speech is right. You cannot be serious. You can play at seriousness. But then you are still playing, even if you are fully taken in by your own game and are, therefore, as player, not taken in. You cannot be serious.

There does not come a time when things get serious. There only comes a time when we seriously play at seriousness. It's a funny game. Not funny-ha-ha; but funny-ironic; because it pretends not to be play.

Sometimes we play so well that we simply forget we are playing. We think our play is reality. It is.

Sometimes we play so badly that we forget we are playing. We think our play is work. It is.

But then if man cannot in fact be serious why does he so often pretend to be? And delude himself in the process? Especially why is this so since man does not enjoy seriousness as much as he enjoys play? It is so simply because—as the author of *The God Game* writes —self-pity is the most delicious of all emotions.

Coomaraswamy once said: "The artist is not a special kind of man, but every man is a special kind of artist." So also: The player and dancer are not special kinds of men, but every man is a special kind of player and dancer. To say "I am not playing" or "I am not pretending" is simply a very clever way of playing and pretending. It is the game we play and the pretense we pretend when, unwittingly and witlessly, we don't want to have fun.

Life is a game. If I had written, "Life is like a game," you would have asked, "Like which game?" Actually it is like the game of life. That's why I wrote, "Life is a game."

Life is a kind of hit-and-run game—according to those who cannot see that life is the game of life. For them it is the end, the purpose, that has value. Not how you play, but whether you win the game. Hit and run. In baseball, hit and run *so* you can get on base. In traffic games, hit and run *so* you can avoid prosecution. Always trying to figure out when to run. And where. Why not hit and run just to hit and run.

What did you do today? I played. What did you play? I just played. Why did you do that? Just for fun.

Musician John Cage tells the following story:

An Indian lady invited me to dinner and said Dr. Suzuki [the famed Zen scholar] would be there. He was. Before dinner I mentioned Gertrude Stein. Suzuki had never heard of her. I described aspects of her work, which he said sounded very interesting. Stimulated, I mentioned James Joyce, whose name was also new to him. At dinner he was unable to eat the curries that were offered, so a few uncooked vegetables and fruits were brought, which he enjoyed. After dinner the talk turned to metaphysical problems, and there were many questions, for the hostess was a follower of a certain Indian yogi and her guests were more or less equally divided between allegiance to Indian thought and to Japanese thought. About eleven o'clock we were out on the street walking along, and an American lady said, "How is it, Dr. Suzuki? We spend the evening asking you questions and nothing is decided." Dr. Suzuki smiled and said, "That's why I love philosophy: no one wins."[2]

Games may well seduce us into purposiveness. Into wanting to win some*thing*. But play: that is a different matter. Play is purposeless. Persons who play games in order to win are not playing games; they are working at them. That's why they do not win.

John Fowles has an aphorism on this point: "Means-orientated societies, for whom the game is the game. Ends-orientated societies, for whom the game is winning. In the first, if one is happy, then one is successful; in the second, one cannot be happy unless one is successful. The whole tendency of evolution and history suggests that man must become means-orientated if he is to survive."[3]

All life is for play: foreplay.

_____

It's not that we should stop working and start playing, but that we should work as if at play, because that is what we are doing anyway: playing at work.

Sometimes, however, it is necessary to stop working for a while and start playing, so that we may stop working at work, and play;

so that we may go back to playing at work, which we were doing in the first place. But we forgot.

The nongoal goal: to become an interior decorator.

But man can no more *make* play than he can *make* love. Why do we say "make love"? Because that is precisely what we do: we game at love, as if our erotic game were love itself, and miracle of miracles, it is. The *as if* is reality. Reality is a play. We do "make love," but not by trying.

Don't try. Just do it. And don't try to "just do it," either. Forget the whole thing.

A pop-song title of several years back: "Shall We Dance?" Answer: not on command, not by trying, but sometimes by chance. Serendipity.

"Look Ma, I'm dancing!" Are you? Certainly you are not dancing the dance you were dancing before you said, "Look Ma, I'm dancing!" Now you are dancing, that's true; but now you are dancing the "Look Ma, I'm dancing" dance.

Can man play? No, not intentionally, not volitionally or rationally. But he cannot not-play either. Play cannot be accomplished, but it always happens. For those who have dancing eyes to see. We must learn not to *do* play, but to *see* the play in it all. But of course we cannot do that either; not by trying. Yet sometimes we do "do" it. Or rather, it happens to us. Like a love affair. It all comes from playing around.

"Tonight we improvise," wrote Pirandello. Let it happen. A happening! "Play it out," says the fisherman, "all the way. Let the poor fish hook himself." Let it happen. "Fairy tales can come true, it can happen to you," sings a popular song. And never forget the childhood wisdom of the nursery rhyme: "Leave them alone and they'll come home."

Not only children, but ancient religious traditions, know this wisdom. "Unless you receive the kingdom of God like a child, you cannot enter into it." A kingdom of play! Theologians have forgotten.

A theology of play might help. But it would not be theo*logy*. It might be more like *theopoiēsis*. Or even *theography*: writing about the gods, like geography, mapping where the gods go, where the spirit is.

A theology of play as theography would view things differently. The old things would seem new.

It would think of resting on the first day of the week rather than the seventh. Leisure, contemplation, holiday, and play do not come at the end of work; they are the bases of all life.

Theography would prefer Mary to Martha, the former being one who sees the practicality of the impractical, the value of playing around.

It would see with Jacob Boehme that Adam fell from paradise when his "play became serious business."

It would understand Sri Ramakrishna's answer to the problem of theodicy. "Why, God being good, is there evil in the world?" "To thicken the plot."

Theography of play would likely think that bearing witness sounds burdensome and plodding, and would therefore hope to bare witness.

And of course it would all likely lead from theography to theograffiti: a theology of the everyday, seeing the spirit of life in all life.

Would you believe "minitheology"?—revealing more with less.

Notes

INTRODUCTION "The Care and Feeding of Hobby Horses"

1. E. E. Calkins, *The Care and Feeding of Hobby Horses* (New York: Leisure League of America, 1934), p. 3.
2. Robert E. Neale, "Religion and Play," *Crossroads* (July-September, 1967), p. 68.

CHAPTER TWO The Contemporary Academic Game of Games

1. Johan Huizinga, *The Waning of the Middle Ages* (Garden City: Doubleday and Company, 1954).
2. Johan Huizinga, *Homo Ludens: A Study of the Play Element in Culture*, trans. R. F. C. Hull (Boston: Beacon Press, 1955), p. 45.
3. Joseph Campbell, *The Masks of God*, vol. 1, *Primitive Mythology* (New York: Viking Press, 1959), p. 21.
4. *Ibid.*, p. 28.

5. Roger Callois, *Man, Play and Games*, trans. Meyer Barash (New York: The Free Press of Glencoe, 1961), p. 36.

6. *Ibid.*, p. 54.

7. *Ibid.*, p. 64.

8. See Chapter 4 for a fuller treatment of Mead's views.

9. Charles H. Cooley has also been credited with originating "play-theory" in sociology, though his work is more distinctly narrowed to the concept of "role." See his *Human Nature and the Social Order* (New York: Charles Scribner's Sons, 1922).

10. Erving Goffman, *The Presentation of Self in Everyday Life* (Garden City: Doubleday and Company, Anchor Books, 1959), p. 253.

11. Erving Goffman, *Interaction Ritual: Essays on Face-to-Face Behavior* (Garden City: Doubleday and Company, Anchor Books, 1967), pp. 149, 150, 151, 152, 154, 155–156.

12. *Ibid.*, p. 194.

13. *Ibid.*, p. 269.

14. See Peter Berger, *The Precarious Vision: A Sociologist Looks at Social Fictions and Christian Faith* (Garden City: Doubleday and Company, 1961), p. 71. See also Berger's book *Rumor of Angels,* published after this work was in the process of publication (Garden City: Doubleday and Company, 1969), which has an extended section on "Play."

15. Nigel Calder, *Eden Was No Garden: An Inquiry into the Environment of Man* (New York: Holt, Rinehart and Winston, 1967), pp. 218–219.

16. *Ibid.*, p. 176.

17. This game has been well analyzed in *The Sex Game,* by JESSIE BERNARD (Englewood Cliffs, N.J.: Prentice-Hall, 1968). The author writes: "All games played by both sexes are, in a general sense, sex games" (p. 304). She identifies "the rock-bottom characterizing nature of the sex-as-fun games: no ties. If it lasts too long, one of the players is almost sure to become bored, or both may. . . . Or one partner falls in love with the other, or they both do. And love is serious. Sex becomes much more than fun. Love spoils the game" (p. 306). The serious/fun dichotomy which here produces a love/sex dichotomy may be dubious, but the author is certainly correct in identifying a revolution in our age's consciousness which implicates,

among many other things, the war between the sexes. "We may be creating," the author writes, "a kind of woman who is satisfied with the touch-and-go, sex-as-fun game. If we are, she is a phenomenon so new that we can hardly even begin to trace the implications either for her or for the family or for the social order" (p. 308). Indeed! One of these "new women" who employs the game terminology is JEANNIE SAKOL. In her book, *The Inept Seducer or Bad Intentions Are Not Enough* (New York: Price, Stern, Sloan, 1968), she has written the following aphorisms about men: "The Winner understands the nature of winning and losing. He knows you can lose by winning and win by losing. The loser doesn't catch on to the nuances of human reaction and is usually either surprised or hurt when his winning ploy turns into a deadly dud." "A Winner talks about public parts of his private life; A Loser talks about the private parts of his public life." "A Loser makes elaborate plans, including sly strategic tricks, to make out with a girl who goes home with everyone. A Winner leaves her politely at the door (but may allow her to drag him inside by the lapels)." "Losers use dirty words. Winners say them with their eyes." No comment!

18. Calder, *Eden Was No Garden*, p. 185.

19. "Adam Smith," *The Money Game* (New York: Random House, 1968), p. 10.

20. *Ibid.*, pp. 300–301, 302.

21. See Berger, *The Precarious Vision*, p. 84.

22. Goffman, *Presentation of Self*, p. 254.

23. H. C. Lehman and P. A. Witty, *The Psychology of Play Activities* (New York: A. S. Barnes, 1927), p. 23, quoting chemist Edwin Slosson.

24. *Ibid.*, p. 23.

25. Jean Piaget, *Play, Dreams and Imitation in Childhood*, trans. C. Gattegno and F. M. Hodgson (New York: W. W. Norton, 1962), p. 168.

26. Arnold R. Beisser, *The Madness in Sports: Psychosocial Observations on Sports* (New York: Appleton-Century-Crofts, 1967), pp. 238–239.

27. Eric Berne, *Games People Play* (New York: Grove Press, 1964), p. 48.

28. A slightly different use of the game/play metaphor (but not *so* different as might appear on first glance) may be observed in the writings of WILLIAM C. SCHUTZ (*Joy: Expanding Human Awareness*, 1967) and BERNARD GUNTHER (*Sense Relaxation: Below Your Mind*, 1968), both of whom are staff members at the Esalen Institute in California. The Institute's goal, as the book titles suggest, is heightened human sensitivity in interpersonal and personal situations. The goal is approached through group-training activities which often employ the designations of "game" or "play," as for example in the case of Schutz's description of "The Fantasy Game" whose purpose is the clarification of "the psychological elements that contribute to a person's conflict" by asking the person to "personify the parts of the conflict" in a game of fantasizing or daydreaming. In fact, the total aim of these books seems to be the cultivation through "group games" of a more playful attitude toward life.

29. Thomas Szasz, *The Myth of Mental Illness* (New York: Dell Publishing Co., Delta Books, 1967), p. 236.

30. *Ibid.*, pp. 234–235.

31. Jay Haley, *Strategies of Psychotherapy* (New York: Grune and Stratton, 1963), pp. 186–187.

32. *Ibid.*, pp. 193, 195–196, 201.

33. Gregory Bateson, "A Theory of Play and Fantasy," *Psychiatric Research Reports*, II (1955), 40–41.

34. See the remarkable book by WILLIAM FRY on theories of humor and laughter which grew out of this research: *Sweet Madness* (Palo Alto: Pacific Books, 1963).

35. See the following articles which are especially relevant to the argument of the present book: Gregory Bateson, "A Theory of Play and Fantasy," *op cit.*; and Jay Haley, "Paradoxes in Play, Fantasy, and Psychotherapy," *Psychiatric Research Reports*, II (1955), 52–58. Also, the entire literature of this research is reviewed by Paul Watzlawick in an article entitled, "A Review of the Double-Bind Theory," in *Family Process*, II, 1 (March, 1963), 132–153.

36. Franz Alexander, "A Contribution to the Theory of Play," *The Psychoanalytic Quarterly*, XXVII (April, 1958), pp. 186–187, 192.

37. Herbert Marcuse, *Eros and Civilization* (New York: Random House, Vintage Books, 1955), p. 178.

38. Erik Erikson, *Childhood and Society* (New York: W. W. Norton, 1950), p. 222.

39. Sigmund Freud, *Beyond the Pleasure Principle* (New York: Bantam Books, 1967), p. 33.

40. Sigmund Freud, *On Creativity and the Unconscious* (New York: Harper & Row, Torchbooks, 1958), p. 54. Also, we should mention, in this final footnote in the psychology section of our review, that two discussions of play have come to our attention after this book was in process of publication, namely: PAUL W. PRUYSER, *A Dynamic Psychology of Religion* (New York: Harper & Row, 1968), pp. 252ff.; and SUSANNA MILLAR, *The Psychology of Play* (Baltimore: Penguin Books, 1968).

41. John Ciardi, "Adam and Eve and the Third Son," *Saturday Review* (August 29, 1964), pp. 142–143, 178.

42. Cited in Joseph Campbell, *The Masks of God,* vol. 4, *Creative Mythology* (New York: Viking Press, 1968), p. 662. See also, the work of ARTHUR KOESTLER on the creative imagination: *The Act of Creation* (New York: The Macmillan Co., 1964), especially the section in Book Two entitled, "Playing and Pretending."

43. W. H. Auden, *The Dyer's Hand* (New York: Random House, Vintage Books, 1968), p. 432.

44. *Ibid.,* pp. 88–89.

45. Geoffrey H. Hartmann, *The Unmediated Vision: An Interpretation of Wordsworth, Hopkins, Rilke, and Valéry* (New York: Harcourt, Brace and World, Harbinger Books, 1966), p. 162. Hartmann traces the origin of this view to nineteenth-century Romanticism, as does Norman O. Brown. See the latter's *Life Against Death* (New York: Random House, Modern Library Paperbacks, 1959), pp. 66f., 73. Also, see MARTIN HEIDEGGER, *Existence and Being,* "Hölderlin and the Essence of Poetry" (Chicago: Henry Regnery, Gateway Editions, 1949), pp. 272ff., 283, 286.

46. The lines are taken from the *Sonnets to Orpheus* (1922), II, 10; I, 3; II, 10; II, 9; see also, II, 8. The translation used here is by

C. F. MacIntyre (Berkeley: University of California Press, 1960), pp. 75, 7, 75, 73.

47. Rainer Maria Rilke, *Duino Elegies*, trans. C. F. MacIntyre (Berkeley: University of California Press, 1965), p. 33.

48. See Hermann Hesse, *Magister Ludi*, trans. M. Savill (New York: Ungar Publishing Co., 1965), p. 39.

49. Martin Esslin, *The Theatre of the Absurd* (Garden City: Doubleday and Company, Anchor Books, 1961), p. 150.

50. Jean Genet, *The Balcony*, trans. B. Frechtman (New York: Grove Press, Evergreen Books, 1958), p. 47.

51. Tom Stoppard, *Rosencrantz and Guildenstern Are Dead* (New York: Grove Press, Evergreen Books, 1967), p. 13.

52. *Ibid.*, pp. 124, 125, 126.

53. Karl A. Olsson, *The God Game* (New York: The World Publishing Company, 1968), p. 154.

54. Edward Albee, *Who's Afraid of Virginia Woolf?* (New York: Atheneum, 1962), p. 117.

55. Samuel Beckett, *Waiting for Godot* (New York: Grove Press, Evergreen Books, 1954), pp. 28–29.

56. Julio Cortázar, *The Winners*, trans. E. Kerrigan (New York: Pantheon Books, 1965), p. 8.

57. Julio Cortázar, *Hopscotch*, trans. G. Rabassa (New York: New American Library, Signet Books, 1967), p. 298.

58. *Ibid.*, p. 441.

59. Julio Cortázar, *End of the Game and Other Stories*, trans. P. Blackburn (New York: Pantheon Books, 1967), pp. 148–149.

60. Josef Pieper, *Leisure: The Basis of Culture*, trans. A. Dru (New York: New American Library, Mentor-Omega Books, 1963), p. 40.

61. *Ibid.*, p. 43.

62. *Ibid.*, pp. 80, 81, 82.

63. There is a work analogous to that of Pieper in contemporary philosophy of education that merits mention. The book is entitled *Work, Leisure, and the American Schools* (New York: Random House, 1968) and is written by the American philosopher of education THOMAS F. GREEN. Green argues that "the underlying metaphors of teaching and schooling can be usefully related to play, even though in practice

they are more closely related to work" (p. 159). "It is perhaps this connection between play and leisure that should give us a major clue as to the form and institutional expression of education for a leisure society. The clue is that, among other things, there must be a stronger expression of the play element in school, which does not mean teaching through games. It means, instead, more explicit attention to the element of play in the learning of languages, history, the social studies, and the sciences. It means a stronger focus on playing with ideas, as well as with one's hands, in order to bring out the intrinsic value and enjoyment of learning. It means viewing the curriculum as essentially a series of jungle-gyms, and teaching as the activity of seducing children into playing on them. . . . The end result, the ultimate product, may be a child who has been inducted into a human community; the immediate goal, however, is to get him to play on the jungle-gym. It is to get him to enjoy using his mind as an historian. I have seen this happen in elementary schools, and the result is electrifying. Understood in this way, learning has its own immediate motivation; it cannot be understood in relation to some remote goal. In this sense, the value of teaching and of learning is like the value of play—intrinsic and immediate" (pp. 160–161).

64. See also R. B. BRAITHWAITE, *Theory of Games as a Tool for the Moral Philosopher* (Cambridge: At the University Press, 1963), which is a quite different and less well-known use of the "game" metaphor in linguistic analytic philosophy.

65. Ludwig Wittgenstein, *Philosophical Investigations,* trans. G. E. M. Anscombe (Oxford: Blackwell; New York: The Macmillan Company, 1953), No. 66.

66. The present author is following a specific line of interpretation with regard to this philosophical game-theory. It is one that has been developed by a philosopher at the University of California at Santa Cruz: see ROBERT GOFF, "The Wittgenstein Game," *The Christian Scholar,* XLV, 3 (Fall, 1962), 179–197. If the reader wishes to consult alternate interpretations of the Wittgensteinian language-game idea, he may consult one of the following: M. J. Charlesworth, *Philosophy and Linguistic Analysis* (Pittsburgh: Duquesne Studies, Philosophical

Series No. 9, 1959); David Pole, *The Later Philosophy of Wittgenstein* (London: University of London, Athlone Press, 1958); and Paul Feyerabend, "Wittgenstein's *Philosophical Investigations*," *Philosophical Review*, LXIV (July, 1955).

67. Goff, "The Wittgenstein Game," *op. cit.*, p. 192.

68. *Ibid.*, p. 193.

69. A note should be added at this point in the review to acknowledge two other thinkers, not themselves linguistic analysts, who have nonetheless contributed significantly to the use of the game/play metaphor in the area of philosophy of language. The first is MAR-SHALL MCLUHAN. See especially his chapter "Games, The Extensions of Man" in *Understanding Media: The Extensions of Man* (New York: McGraw-Hill Book Co., 1965), pp. 234–245; his section on "play" in *The Gutenberg Galaxy* (Toronto: University of Toronto Press, 1962), pp. 188–191; and the entire playful book, written with Quentin Fiore, *The Medium Is the Massage: An Inventory of Effects* (New York: Bantam Books, 1967). The second thinker who should be acknowledged at this point is WILLIAM STEPHENSON. His book, *The Play Theory of Mass Communication* (Chicago: University of Chicago Press, 1967), is rigorous and careful in its application of the play metaphor to principles of communication. It represents an important attempt to disengage communications theory from the stronghold of those who feel that the only purpose of language is to purvey information and data. The argument on behalf of "play" is incisively developed and could revolutionize the television, radio, newspaper, and publishing industries if it were taken "seriously."

70. Both taken from Eugen Fink, *Le Jeu comme symbole du monde*, trans. H. Hildebrand and A. Lindenberg, Arguments, 29 (Paris: Éditions de Minuit, 1966), pp. 63, 64 (present author's translation).

71. Theodor Haecker, "Wahrheit und Leben," *Essays* (Munich: Kösel Verlag, 1958), p. 303 (present author's translation).

72. Hans-Georg Gadamer, *Wahrheit und Methode: Grundzüge einer philosophischen Hermeneutik*, 2nd ed. (Tübingen: J. C. B. Mohr, 1965), p. 97.

73. In *Wesen und Sinn des Spiels* [The Essence and Significance of Play] (Berlin: Kurt Wolff Verlag, 1933), p. 129 (present author's translation).

74. Haecker, "Wahrheit und Leben," *op. cit.*, p. 303 (present author's translation).

75. Gadamer, *Wahrheit und Methode*, pp. 98, 97–98, 97.

76. Fink, *Le Jeu*, pp. 227, 238.

77. *Ibid.*, p. 63.

78. Eugen Fink, *Oase des Glücks: Gedanken zu einer Ontologie des Spiels* [Oasis of Fortune: Thoughts toward an Ontology of Play] (Freiburg/Munich: Karl Alber Verlag, 1957), p. 51. See also the contribution to philosophical play-theory by INGEBORG HEIDEMANN: "Philosophische Theorien des Spiels," *Kant-Studien*, L (1958–1959), 316–322. Heidemann, like Fink, is inquiring into the possibility of using the metaphor of play for a conceptual model in a new metaphysics (*der Spielbegriff wird zum Modellbegriff der Metaphysik*). A slightly different but equally important contribution is made by GERHARD VON KUJAWA in *Ursprung und Sinn des Spiels* (Cologne: E. A. Seeman Verlag, 1949).

79. *Two-Person Game Theory: The Essential Ideas* (Ann Arbor: University of Michigan Press, Ann Arbor Science Paperbacks, 1966), p. 14.

80. *Ibid.*, p. 17.

81. *Ibid.*, p. 214.

82. Robert S. DeRopp, *The Master Game: Pathways to Higher Consciousness beyond the Drug Experience* (New York: Delacorte Press, Seymour Lawrence Book, 1968), p. 11.

83. *Ibid.*, p. 13.

84. *Ibid.*, p. 19.

85. Alan Watts, *Beyond Theology: The Art of Godmanship* (New York: Pantheon Books, 1964), pp. 31–32, 54.

86. Hugo Rahner, S. J., *Man at Play*, trans. B. Battershaw and E. Quinn (New York: Herder and Herder, 1967), pp. 65–66. Used by permission.

87. Eleanor S. Morrison, "Leisure, Worship, and Play," *Crossroads* (March, 1966), p. 12. Credit should be given to a scholar who argued for the conception of liturgy as play long before either Rahner or Morrison. The European Roman Catholic theologian ROMANO GUARDINI published a normative work on the meaning of worship in 1935. It was titled *The Church and the Catholic and the Spirit of the Liturgy* (New York: Sheed and Ward, 1935). On p. 179 of that

book is to be found the following definition of liturgy: "a kind of holy play in which the soul, with utter abandonment, learns how to waste time for the sake of God."

88. Robert E. Neale, "Religion and Play," *Crossroads* (July-September, 1967), p. 93. It should be mentioned that Neale's view on the formal similarity between religious festivals (i.e., ritual) and human play is disputed by the formidable European historian of religions CARL KERENYI. In *The Religion of the Greeks and Romans* (New York: E. P. Dutton and Co., 1962), Kerenyi argues that "playful existence is happier and less substantial than the festive." He says: "The festive atmosphere alternates between the serious and the playful, between close constraint and absolute freedom" (p. 64). Clearly Kerenyi and Neale have conceived the structure of play differently. The dispute should not be taken lightly because Kerenyi's history-of-religions reservation about the play metaphor occurs as a theological disclaimer in the thought of the Danish theologian SØREN KIERKEGAARD. In the *Edifying Discourses*, Kierkegaard argues against making the play of children into a religious ideal, a viewpoint which he sees as being regressive and as putting the religious man in the same position as Lot's wife who by looking back was turned into a rigid pillar. Something not to be taken lightly!

89. Gerardus van der Leeuw, *Sacred and Profane Beauty: The Holy in Art*, trans. D. F. Green (New York: Holt, Rinehart and Winston, 1963), p. 86.

90. *Ibid.*, pp. 111–112. See also the theology of art which utilizes the play metaphor by DAVID B. HARNED, *Theology and the Arts* (Philadelphia: Westminster Press, 1966), especially pp. 168ff.

91. Sister Corita, *Footnotes and Headlines: A Play-Pray Book* (New York: Herder and Herder, 1967), pp. 4, 26, 40. Used by permission.

92. Douglas J. Stewart, "The Humanities, the Whore and the Alderman," *AAUP Bulletin*, LI, 1 (Autumn, 1965), 359.

CHAPTER THREE   *The Origin and History of Ideas about Games and Play*

1. See Giambattista Vico, *The New Science of Giambattista Vico*, trans. T. Bergin and M. Fisch (Garden City: Doubleday and Company,

Anchor Books, 1961), especially the chapter entitled "Epitomes of Poetic History," pp. 208–211.

2. Much of this is borrowed from a colleague, Dr. James B. Wiggins, a religious historian who has stimulated, indeed has suggested, many of these historiographical opinions. The present author is therefore entirely in the debt of Professor Wiggins for this "play-theory" of history.

3. John Barth, *Lost in a Funhouse* (Garden City: Doubleday and Company, 1968), pp. 1–2.

4. Alan Watts, *The Book: On the Taboo against Knowing Who You Are* (New York: Pantheon Books, 1966), pp. 13–14.

5. Nietzsche's tracing of the Orphic source of this Heraclitean aphorism is found in his *Philosophy in the Tragic Age of the Greeks*. See also, W. K. C. Guthrie, *Orpheus and Greek Religion: A Study of the Orphic Movement* (New York: W. W. Norton, 1966), especially pp. 89, 98, 120, 203; and Hugo Rahner, S.J., *Man At Play* (New York: Herder and Herder, 1967), p. 17, which has a notation about a Theban myth that refers to Dionysos' play.

6. *Vitae et Placita Philosophorum*, IX.1.17.

7. *Geography*, XVI.29.

8. The present author is greatly indebted in this chapter to the researches of Johan Huizinga (*Homo Ludens: A Study of the Play Element in Culture*. Boston: Beacon Press, 1955) and Hugo Rahner (*Man at Play*). The specific reference to the etymologies cited is found in the Huizinga book on pp. 30–31, 38–40, 43; see also Huizinga's conclusions regarding the significance of these etymologies on pp. 44–45. For a rather different conclusion about the same etymologies, see Theodore Thass-Thienemann, *The Subconscious Language* (New York: Washington Square Press, 1967), pp. 341–346.

9. *Epistle*, VI.323D, cited from *Plato's Epistles*, trans. G. R. Morrow. (Indianapolis: Bobbs-Merrill Co., Library of Liberal Arts, 1962), p. 214.

10. *Laws*, III.685A, cited from *The Dialogues of Plato*, trans. B. Jowett, 3rd ed. (Oxford: Clarendon Press, 1892), V, 65.

11. *Republic*, X.604.

12. See Eric Voegelin, *Order and History*, vol. 3, *Plato and Aristotle*. (Baton Rouge: Louisiana State University Press, 1957), pp. 183ff.

Voegelin writes: "The symbols [of myth], therefore, do not denote an unconscious reality as an object, but, rather, are the unconscious reality itself, broken in the medium of consciousness. The freedom of the play is possible only as long as the creator of a myth remains aware of the character of the symbols as a nonobjective reality in objective form. If he loses the sense that dangerous forces are playing through him when he plays with the myth, when perhaps he goes out in search of the object expressed in symbols, or attempts to prove or disprove its existence, not only his labors will be lost, but he may lose his soul in the process" (p. 192). See also, Gavin Ardley, "The Role of Play in the Philosophy of Plato," *Philosophy*, XLII, 42 (July, 1967), 226–244; and Walter Kaufmann, *Critique of Religion and Philosophy* (New York: Harper & Brothers, 1958), pp. 9–10, which is a section entitled "Why Most Philosophers Cannot Laugh."

13. See *Laws*, I.643C; VII.803; also, *Republic*, IV.424; VII.537.

14. The thesis of Gavin Ardley's article, mentioned in note 12, is somewhat in opposition to the argument presented here. Ardley is concerned, as is the present author, with "healing the play/serious dualism" (*op. cit.*, p. 226). But unlike our argument, Ardley attempts to make the case for play by way of the philosophy of Plato. Our evaluation of Plato in the history of the idea of play is more akin to that of Eugen Fink. See his book *Le Jeu comme symbole du monde*, trans. H. Hildenbrand and A. Lindenberg (Paris: Les Éditions de Minuit, 1966).

15. *Commentary on Matthew*, Homily 6.6, cited in Rahner, *Man at Play*, p. 98.

16. *Enarrationes in Psalmos*, 127.15, cited in Rahner, *Man at Play*, p. 41.

17. Cited in Karl Groos, *The Play of Man*, trans. E. L. Baldwin (New York: D. Appleton and Co., 1901), pp. 398–399.

18. Cited from Paul Lauter, ed., *Theories of Comedy* (Garden City: Doubleday and Company, Anchor Books, 1964), p. 137.

19. *Comm. in Proverbia*, 8.31, cited in Rahner, *Man at Play*, p. 23.

20. *Carmina*, 1.2.2, vv. 589–590, cited in Rahner, *Man at Play*, p. 23.

21. *Ambigua*, 263a, cited in Rahner, *Man at Play*, pp. 24–25.

22. Cited in Rahner, *Man at Play*, p. 10.

23. *Paedagogus*, 1.5.22.1, cited in Rahner, *Man at Play*, p. 49.

24. See Rahner, *Man at Play*, pp. 54, 58.

25. *Commentarii in Zachariam*, 11.8, cited in Rahner, *Man at Play*, p. 51.

26. Cited in Huizinga, *Homo Ludens*, p. 212n.

27. For a somewhat different interpretation of Aristotle's notion of *eutrapelia*, see Ardley, "The Role of Play," *op. cit.* For Thomas' own thoughts, see *Summa Theologica*, Pr. 11–11, Quest. 168, Articles 2–4. It is on this latter that our own interpretation is dependent.

28. The phrases are Robert E. Neale's. See his "Religion and Play," *Crossroads* (July-September, 1967), pp. 71ff.

29. "Heil dem Geist, der uns verbinden mag; / den wir leben wahrhaft in Figuren." *Sonnets to Orpheus*, trans. C. F. MacIntyre. (Berkeley: University of California Press, 1960), pp. 24–25 (I.12).

30. Robert Neale, "Religion and Play," *op. cit.*, p. 93.

31. Friedrich Nietzsche, *Ecce Homo*, No. 10, in G. Clive, *The Philosophy of Nietzsche* (New York: New American Library, Mentor Books, 1965), p. 65.

32. *Kosmiche Liturgie. Maximus der Bekenner, Höhe und Krise des griechischen Weltbildes* (Freiburg, 1941), pp. 7–8; cited in Rahner, *Man at Play*, p. 25.

CHAPTER FOUR   *The Origin and History of the Spirit of Play in Man*

1. See Joseph Campbell, "Bios and Mythos: Prolegomena to a Science of Mythology," Wilbur and Muensterberger, eds., *Psychology and Culture: Essays in Honor of Géza Roheim* (New York: International Universities Press, 1951), pp. 329–343.

2. The correspondence between the history of man's ideas and his own growth and development has been argued compellingly in the work of Erich Neumann, *The Origins and History of Consciousness*, trans. R. F. C. Hull (New York: Harper & Row, Torchbooks, 1962), 2 vols. See also, Norman O. Brown, *Life against Death* (New York:

Random House, 1959), especially pp. 13ff.; and Owen Barfield, *Saving the Appearances: A Study in Idolatry* (London: Faber and Faber, 1957). In the latter book the case is made, similar to that of Neumann, that the origin and history of consciousness is the story of the loss of an original unity, followed by a process of differentiation, leading ultimately to the need for reintegration. Thus, the stories being rehearsed in this chapter and in the last one are neither new nor unique in the present author's understanding. Rather, the old, old story told by so many is simply being retold in the categories of play and games.

3. See Sigmund Freud, *A General Introduction to Psychoanalysis* (New York: Washington Square Press, 1961), pp. 219, 312–328; and Norman O. Brown, *Life against Death*, pp. 23–39. The interpretations presented in the latter work have greatly influenced the present argument.

4. See Erich Neumann, *The Origins and History of Consciousness*, I, 11; cf. *ibid.*, II, 261–356.

5. See Carl G. Jung, *Psyche and Symbol*, ed. V. S. de Laszlo (Garden City: Doubleday and Company, Anchor Books, 1958), pp. 1–60.

6. Jean Piaget, *Play, Dreams and Imitation in Childhood,* trans. C. Gattegno and F. M. Hodgson. (New York: W. W. Norton, 1962), p. 168; see also all of Part II, pp. 87–212.

7. Erik Erikson, *Childhood and Society,* 2nd ed. (New York: W. W. Norton, 1963), p. 222, see also pp. 209–246.

8. See, for example, S. S. Boocock and E. O. Schild, *Simulation Games in Learning* (Beverly Hills: Sage Publications, n.d.); and John Holt, *How Children Learn* (New York: Pittman Publishing Corp., 1967).

9. See George Herbert Mead, *Mind, Self, and Society* (Chicago: University of Chicago Press, 1934), pp. 152–163.

10. Joseph Campbell, *Masks of God: Primitive Mythology* (New York: Viking Press, 1959), p. 29, see also p. 23.

11. John Ciardi, "Aphorisms and Doodles," *Saturday Review* (May 21, 1966), p. 8.

12. Cited from Robert Paul Smith, *"Where Did You Go?" "Out." "What Did You Do?" "Nothing."* (New York: Pocket Books, Cardinal Edition, 1959), pp. 98, 105.

13. Simone de Beauvoir, *Pyrrhus et Cinéas* (Paris: Gallimard, 1944), pp. 9f.
14. Dr. Seuss, *The Cat in the Hat Comes Back!* (New York: Random House, Beginner Books, 1958), pp. 3, 10, 12.
15. 1 Corinthians 13:11 (RSV).
16. This apt comparison of Dantean and Hindu ideals is original with Joseph Campbell. See *The Masks of God*, vol. 4, *Creative Mythology* (New York: Viking Press, 1968), pp. 633–634.
17. John Cage, *Silence* (Cambridge, Mass.: MIT Press, 1961), p. 271.
18. See Norman O. Brown, *Life against Death*, Chaps. XII and XVI.

CHAPTER FIVE   *Play Is Religion*

1. Alan Watts, *Beyond Theology: The Art of Godmanship* (New York: Pantheon Books, 1964), p. 29.
2. The "Iron Curtain" illustration is borrowed from: Julián Marías, "Philosophic Truth and the Metaphoric System," S. R. Hopper and D. L. Miller, eds., *Interpretation: The Poetry of Meaning* (New York: Harcourt, Brace and World, Harbinger Book, 1967), pp. 48–49. For a lucid and complete presentation of the dynamics of development from image, to metaphor, to symbol, to myth, to meaning, see Philip Wheelwright, *Metaphor and Reality* (Bloomington: Indiana University Press, 1962).
3. See, for example, Eric Larrabee and Rolf Meyerson, eds., *Mass Leisure* (Glencoe: The Free Press, 1958); Sebastian de Grazia, *Of Time, Work, and Leisure* (Garden City: Doubleday and Company, Anchor Books, 1962); and Charles K. Brightbill, *The Challenge of Leisure* (Englewood Cliffs, N.J.: Prentice-Hall, Spectrum Book, 1960).
4. For another treatment of this same argument, see Northrop Frye, *The Educated Imagination* (Bloomington: Indiana University Press, 1964), Chap. 1.
5. See Rollo May, *Psychology and the Human Dilemma* (Princeton: D. Van Nostrand Co., 1967), Chaps. 1–4.
6. Joseph Campbell, *The Masks of God*, vol. 3, *Occidental Mythology* (New York: Viking Press, 1964), pp. 518–523. See also, Joseph Camp-

bell, *The Masks of God: Creative Mythology* (New York: Viking Press, 1968), pp. 608–624.

7. The conception of the "four marks" was born in the work of a philosopher of religion at Hartford Seminary Foundation. The present author is therefore indebted to Dr. Richard A. Underwood for certain aspects of the format of this section.

8. *Phaedo*, IIIb.

9. Tom Jones, *The Fantasticks* (New York: Drama Book Shop, 1964), p. 28.

10. Joyce Cary, *The Horse's Mouth* (New York: Harper & Row, Perennial Library, 1965), pp. 98–99. Used by permission.

11. Robert E. Neale, "Religion and Play," *Crossroads* (July-September, 1967), pp. 77–78.

12. See Owen Barfield, *Saving the Appearances* (New York: Harcourt, Brace and World, Harbinger Book, 1965).

13. Martin Heidegger, *Existence and Being*, trans. Werner Brock (Chicago: Henry Regnery, Gateway Books, 1949), p. 282.

14. Hans Vaihinger, *The Philosophy of "As-If,"* trans. C. K. Ogden (New York: Barnes and Noble, 1924).

15. See Friedrich Nietzsche, "On Truth and Lie in an Extra-Moral Sense," in Walter Kaufmann, ed., *The Portable Nietzsche* (New York: Viking Press, 1954), pp. 42–47.

16. Beda Allemann, "Metaphor and Antimetaphor," Hopper and Miller, eds., *Interpretation*, pp. 106–107.

17. Carl G. Jung, *Modern Man in Search of a Soul*, trans. W. S. Dell and C. F. Baynes (New York: Harcourt, Brace and World, Harvest Book, 1933), pp. 224–225. Perhaps the subtlest statement on the dynamics of fiction was written by the ancient rhetorician Donatus: "Counterfeit [*falsum*] is the dissembling of fact [*factum*], a lie [*vanum*] is what cannot happen, a fiction [*fictum*] is what is not fact but could happen. A counterfeit is a feigned untruth similar to the truth, a lie is neither possible nor verisimilar, a fiction is wholly without truth but verisimilar. To utter a counterfeit is deceptive, a fiction clever, a falsehood stupid. To utter a counterfeit is a fault, a fiction an ingenuity, a lie a folly. We are deceived by counterfeits, we are delighted by fictions, we despise lies." Cited in Marvin T.

Herrick, *Comic Theory in the Sixteenth Century* (Urbana: University of Illinois Press, Illini Books, 1964), p. 65.

18. See Martin Esslin, "Pataphysical Saint," *The New Statesman* (October 25, 1968).

19. Norman O. Brown, *Love's Body* (New York: Random House, 1966), pp. 245–247.

20. Robert E. Neale, "Religion and Play," *op. cit.*, pp. 94–95.

21. John Fowles, *The Aristos: A Self-Portrait in Ideas* (Boston: Little, Brown, 1964), p. 35. Used by permission.

22. Martin Heidegger, *Discourse on Thinking: A Translation of Gelassenheit*, trans. J. M. Anderson and E. H. Freund. (New York: Harper & Row, 1966), see especially pp. 22–23, 54–57, 68.

23. Eugen Fink, *Le Jeu comme symbole du monde*, trans. H. Hildebrand and A. Lindenberg, Arguments, 29 (Paris: Éditions de Minuit, 1966), p. 239, translation by present author. Also relevant to this section on *therapeia* is Philip Rieff, *The Triumph of the Therapeutic* (New York: Harper & Row, 1966), p. 251: "What . . . should churchmen do? The answer returns clearly: become, avowedly, therapists, administrating a therapeutic institution—under the justificatory mandate that Jesus himself was the first therapeutic."

24. Joseph Campbell, *The Masks of God*, vol. 1, *Primitive Mythology* (New York: Viking Press, 1959), p. 12.

25. Marshall McLuhan, *Understanding Media: The Extensions of Man* (New York: McGraw-Hill Paperbacks, 1965), p. 238.

26. Northrop Frye, *The Modern Century* (Toronto: Oxford University Press, 1967), pp. 87–123.

27. Joachim Wach, *The Comparative Study of Religions* (New York: Columbia University Press, 1961), p. 65.

28. Joseph Campbell, *The Hero with a Thousand Faces* (New York: The World Publishing Co., Meridian Books, 1966), pp. 390–391, 386.

CHAPTER SIX   *Religion Is Play*

1. See Harvey Cox, "The Secular Search for Religious Experience," *Theology Today*, XXV, 3 (October, 1968), 331–332.

2. Hugo Rahner, S.J., *Man at Play* (New York: Herder and Herder, 1967), p. 10.

3. See above, pp. 85–86.

4. Rahner, *Man at Play*, p. 10.

5. Romano Guardini, *The Church and the Catholic and the Spirit of the Liturgy* (New York: Sheed and Ward, 1935), p. 179.

6. See above, pp. 109–110.

7. *Opusc.* lxviii, *in libr. Boetii de Hebdon;* cited in Alan Watts, *Beyond Theology: The Art of Godmanship* (New York: Pantheon Books, 1964), p. 52.

8. Cited by Robert A. Durr, "Life as Play," *Ergo: Supplement to The Daily Orange,* Syracuse, New York, October 6, 1967, p. 5.

9. This is one of the major reasons for the emergence of American graduate studies in religion and literature, an outgrowth of the *Kulturtheologie* of Paul Tillich.

10. Cited by Konrad Lorenz, *On Aggression,* trans. M. K. Wilson. (New York: Bantam Books, 1967), pp. 283–284.

11. Matthew 13:34 (RSV).

12. Matthew 13:10–11a, 13 (RSV).

13. 1 Corinthians 2:13 (RSV, alternate reading).

14. For overviews of the recent discussions of theological method, see Stanley R. Hopper and David L. Miller, eds., *Interpretation: The Poetry of Meaning* (New York: Harcourt, Brace and World, Harbinger Books, 1967), especially the "Introduction"; and Robert Funk, *Language, Hermeneutic, and Word of God* (New York: Harper & Row, 1967), especially Part One.

15. See Philip Wheelwright, *Heraclitus* (New York: Atheneum, 1964).

16. See Donald Frame's "Introduction" to *The Complete Essays of Montaigne,* vol. I, trans. D. Frame (Garden City: Doubleday and Company, Anchor Books, 1960), pp. v–xviii.

17. See J. P. Stern, *Lichtenberg: A Doctrine of Scattered Occasions* (Bloomington: Indiana University Press, 1959).

18. See Robert Goff, "The Wittgenstein Game," *The Christian Scholar,* XLV, 3 (Fall, 1962), 179–197.

19. Stern, *Lichtenberg*, pp. 210, 218, 216.

20. Wheelwright, *Heraclitus*, pp. 58, 102.

21. Ludwig Wittgenstein, *Philosophical Investigations*, trans. G. E. M. Anscombe (Oxford: Blackwell, 1953), Nos. 455–457.

22. See Nikolaus von Kues, *Philosophisch-Theologische Schriften*, vol. 3 (Vienna: Verlag Herder, 1967), pp. 221–355; or *Oeuvres Choisies de Nicolas de Cues*, trans. M. de Gandillac (Aubier: Éditions Montaigne, 1942), pp. 515–539, estraits.

23. Karl Jaspers, *The Great Philosophers*, trans. R. Mannheim (New York: Harcourt, Brace and World, Helen and Kurt Wolff Book, 1966), p. 210.

24. *Kierkegaard's Concluding Unscientific Postscript*, trans. D. Swenson and W. Lowrie (Princeton: Princeton University Press, 1941), p. 235. See also, Stanley R. Hopper, "The Author in Search of His Anecdote," Roger Shinn, ed., *Restless Adventure: Essays on Contemporary Expressions of Existentialism* (New York: Charles Scribner's Sons, 1968), p. 114.

25. *Stromata*, VII.4.

26. *Ibid.*, V.9.

27. Robert E. Neale, "Religion and Play," *Crossroads* (July-September, 1967), p. 84.

28. *Ibid.*, p. 89.

29. Leo Frobenius, *Paideuma, Umrisse einer Kultur- und Seelen-lehre*, 3rd ed. (Frankfurt, 1928), pp. 143–145; cited by Joseph Campbell, *The Masks of God*, vol. 1, *Primitive Mythology* (New York: Viking Press, 1959), p. 22.

30. For a contemporary philosophical statement about the metaphysics of make-believe, see Martin Heidegger, *Being and Time*, trans. J. Macquarrie and E. Robinson (New York: Harper & Row, 1962), pp. 188ff. Two useful expositions of the Heideggerian points are Hopper and Miller, eds., *Interpretation*, p. xvi; and Robert Funk, *Language, Hermeneutic, and Word of God*, p. 231.

31. Mark 9:24 (RSV).

32. Campbell, *The Masks of God*, vol. 1, *Primitive Mythology*, pp. 28–29.

EPILOGUE　*Beyond the Rules of the Religious Game toward a Theology of Play, by Play, and for Play*

1. Piet Hein, *Grooks* (Cambridge, Mass.: MIT Press, 1966), p. 3.
2. John Cage, *Silence* (Cambridge, Mass.: MIT Press, 1961), p. 40. Compare Cage's own thoughts about creative musicology: "And what is the purpose of writing music? One is, of course, not dealing with purposes but dealing with sounds. Or the answer must take the form of paradox: a purposeful purposelessness or a purposeless play. This play, however, is an affirmation of life—not an attempt to bring order out of chaos nor to suggest improvements in creation, but simply a way of waking up to the very life we're living, which is so excellent once one gets one's mind and one's desires out of its way and lets it act of its own accord" (*ibid.*, p. 12).
3. John Fowles, *The Aristos: A Self-Portrait in Ideas* (Boston: Little, Brown, 1964), p. 196.

Bibliography

ALBEE, EDWARD. *Who's Afraid of Virginia Woolf?* New York: Atheneum, 1962.

ALEXANDER, FRANZ. "A Contribution to the Theory of Play." *The Psychoanalytic Quarterly,* XXVII (April, 1958).

AQUINAS, THOMAS. *Summa Theologica.* Trans. Fathers of the English Dominican Province. New York: Benziger Bros., 1947.

ARDLEY, GAVIN. "The Role of Play in the Philosophy of Plato." *Philosophy,* XLII, 42 (July, 1967).

ARISTOTLE. *The Ethics.* Trans. J. A. K. Thomson. Baltimore: Penguin Books, 1958.

AUDEN, W. H. *The Dyer's Hand.* New York: Random House, 1962.

BARFIELD, OWEN. *Saving the Appearances: A Study in Idolatry.* London: Faber and Faber, 1957.

BARTH, JOHN. *Lost in a Funhouse.* Garden City: Doubleday and Company, 1968.

BATESON, GREGORY. "A Theory of Play and Fantasy." *Psychiatric Research Reports,* II (1955).

————— and JURGEN RUESCH. *Communication: The Social Matrix of Psychiatry.* New York: W. W. Norton, 1951.

BECKETT, SAMUEL. *Endgame*. New York: Grove Press, 1958.

———. *Waiting for Godot*. New York: Grove Press, 1954.

BEISSER, ARNOLD. *The Madness in Sports*. New York: Appleton-Century-Crofts, 1967.

BERGER, PETER. *The Precarious Vision*. Garden City: Doubleday and Company, 1961.

BERNARD, JESSIE. *The Sex Game*. Englewood Cliffs, N.J.: Prentice-Hall, 1968.

BERNE, ERIC. *Games People Play*. New York: Grove Press, 1964.

BORGES, JORGE LUIS. *Other Inquisitions, 1937–1952*. New York: Washington Square Press, 1966.

BRACKMAN, JACOB. "The Put-On." *The New Yorker*, XLIII (June 24, 1967).

BRAITHWAITE, R. B. *Theory of Games as a Tool for the Moral Philosopher*. Cambridge: At the University Press, 1963.

BRIGHTBILL, CHARLES. *The Challenge of Leisure*. Englewood Cliffs, N.J.: Prentice-Hall, 1960.

BROWN, NORMAN O. *Life against Death*. New York: Random House, 1959.

———. *Love's Body*. New York: Random House, 1966.

BUYTENDIJK, FRIEDRICH J. J. *Wesen und Sinn des Spiels*. Berlin: Kurt Wolff Verlag, 1933.

CAGE, JOHN. *Silence*. Cambridge, Mass.: MIT Press, 1961.

CALDER, NIGEL. *Eden Was No Garden*. New York: Holt, Rinehart and Winston, 1967.

CALKINS, E. E. *The Care and Feeding of Hobby Horses*. New York: Leisure League of America, 1934.

CALLOIS, ROGER. *Man, Play and Games*. Trans. Meyer Barash. New York: The Free Press of Glencoe, 1961.

CAMPBELL, JOSEPH. "Bios and Mythos." *Psychology and Culture*. Edited by Wilbur and Muensterberger. New York: International Universities Press, 1951.

———. *The Hero with a Thousand Faces*. New York: The World Publishing Company, 1966.

———. *The Masks of God*. 4 vols. New York: Viking Press, 1959–1968.

Vol. 1, *Primitive Mythology*, 1959. Vol. 3, *Occidental Mythology*, 1964. Vol. 4, *Creative Mythology*, 1968.

CARY, JOYCE. *The Horse's Mouth*. New York: Harper & Row, 1965.

CHAPMAN, A. H. *Put-Offs and Come-Ons: Psychological Maneuvers*. New York: G. P. Putnam and Co., 1968.

CIARDI, JOHN. "Adam and Eve and the Third Son." *Saturday Review* (August 29, 1964).

———. "Aphorisms and Doodles." *Saturday Review* (May 21, 1966).

———. "No Subject." *Saturday Review* (August 27, 1966).

CLAPARÈDE, ÉDOUARD. *Experimental Pedagogy and the Psychology of the Child*. Trans. M. Louch and H. Holman. London: Edward Arnold, 1911.

CLEMENT OF ALEXANDRIA. *Selections from the Protreptikos*. Trans. T. Merton. New York: New Directions, 1962.

CLIVE, G. *The Philosophy of Nietzsche*. New York: New American Library, 1965.

COOLEY, CHARLES. *Human Nature and the Social Order*. New York: Charles Scribner's Sons, 1922.

CORITA, SISTER. *Footnotes and Headlines: A Play-Pray Book*. New York: Herder and Herder, 1967.

CORTÁZAR, JULIO. *End of the Game and Other Stories*. Trans. P. Blackburn. New York: Pantheon Books, 1967.

———. *Hopscotch*. Trans. G. Rabassa. New York: New American Library, 1967.

———. *The Winners*. Trans. E. Kerrigan. New York: Pantheon Books, 1965.

COX, HARVEY. "The Secular Search for Religious Experience." *Theology Today*, XXV, 3 (October, 1968).

DE BEAUVOIR, SIMONE. *Pyrrhus et Cinéas*. Paris: Gallimard, 1944.

DE GRAZIA, SEBASTIAN. *Of Time, Work, and Leisure*. Garden City: Doubleday and Company, 1962.

DEROPP, ROBERT. *The Master Game: Pathways to Higher Consciousness beyond the Drug Experience*. New York: Delacorte Press, 1968.

DE ROUGEMENT, DENIS. "Religion and the Mission of the Artist." *Spiritual Problems in Contemporary Literature*. Edited by Stanley R. Hopper. New York: Harper & Row, 1957.

DURRELL, LAWRENCE. *Clea*. New York: Pocket Books, 1961.

ERIKSON, ERIK. *Childhood and Society*. New York: W. W. Norton, 1950.

ESSLIN, MARTIN. "Pataphysical Saint." *The New Statesman* (October 25, 1968).

———. *The Theatre of the Absurd*. Garden City: Doubleday and Company, 1961.

FEYERABEND, PAUL. "Wittgenstein's *Philosophical Investigations*." *Philosophical Review*, LXIV (July, 1955).

FINK, EUGEN. *Le Jeu comme symbole du monde*. Trans. H. Hildebrand and A. Lindenberg. Paris: Éditions de Minuit, 1966.

———. *Oase des Glücks: Gedanken zu einer Ontologie des Spiels*. Freiburg/Munich: Karl Alber Verlag, 1957.

FLAUBERT, GUSTAVE. "Art without Conclusions." *The Modern Tradition: Backgrounds of Modern Literature*. Edited by Richard Ellmann and Charles Feidelson, Jr. New York: Oxford University Press, 1965.

FOWLES, JOHN. *The Aristos: A Self-Portrait in Ideas*. Boston: Little, Brown, 1964.

FREUD, SIGMUND. *Beyond the Pleasure Principle*. New York: Bantam Books, 1967.

———. *A General Introduction to Psychoanalysis*. New York: Washington Square Press, 1961.

———. "The Relation of the Poet to Day-Dreaming." *On Creativity and the Unconscious*. New York: Harper & Row, 1958.

FRY, WILLIAM. *Sweet Madness*. Palo Alto: Pacific Books, 1963.

FRYE, NORTHROP. *The Educated Imagination*. Bloomington: Indiana University Press, 1964.

———. *The Modern Century*. Toronto: Toronto University Press, 1967.

FUNK, ROBERT. *Language, Hermeneutic, and Word of God*. New York: Harper & Row, 1967.

GADAMER, HANS-GEORG. *Wahrheit und Methode*. Tübingen: J. C. B. Mohr, 1965.

GENET, JEAN. *The Balcony*. Trans. B. Frechtman. New York: Grove Press, 1958.

GOFF, ROBERT. "The Wittgenstein Game." *The Christian Scholar,* XLV, 3 (Fall, 1962).

GOFFMAN, ERVING. *Encounters.* Indianapolis: Bobbs-Merrill Co., 1961.

———. *Interaction Ritual.* Garden City: Doubleday and Company, 1967.

———. *The Presentation of Self in Everyday Life.* Garden City: Doubleday and Company, 1959.

GRAHAM, AELRED. *Zen Catholicism.* New York: Harcourt, Brace and World, 1963.

The Greek Anthology. Trans. W. R. Patton. New York: G. P. Putnam Co., 1926.

GREEN, THOMAS. *Work, Leisure, and the American Schools.* New York: Random House, 1968.

GROOS, KARL. *The Play of Man.* Trans. E. L. Baldwin. New York: D. Appleton and Co., 1901.

GROTJAHN, MARTIN. *Beyond Laughter.* New York: McGraw-Hill Book Co., 1957.

GUARDINI, ROMANO. *The Church and the Catholic and the Spirit of the Liturgy.* New York: Sheed and Ward, 1935.

GUNTHER, BERNARD. *Sense Relaxation: Below Your Mind.* New York: Collier Books, 1968.

GUTHRIE, W. K. C. *Orpheus and Greek Religion.* New York: W. W. Norton, 1966.

HAECKER, THEODOR. "Wahrheit und Leben." *Essays.* Munich: Kösel Verlag, 1958.

HALEY, JAY. "Paradoxes in Play, Fantasy, and Psychotherapy." *Psychiatric Research Reports,* II (1955).

———. *Strategies of Psychotherapy.* New York: Grune and Stratton, 1963.

HARNED, DAVID. *Theology and the Arts.* Philadelphia: Westminster Press, 1966.

HARTMANN, GEOFFREY. *The Unmediated Vision.* New York: Harcourt, Brace and World, 1966.

HEIDEGGER, MARTIN. *Being and Time.* Trans. J. Macquarrie and E. Robinson. New York: Harper & Row, 1962.

———— . *Discourse on Thinking.* Trans. J. M. Anderson and E. H. Freund. New York: Harper & Row, 1966.

———— . *Existence and Being.* Trans. W. Brock. Chicago: Henry Regnery, 1949.

———— . *Unterwegs zur Sprache.* Pfullingen: Verlag Günther Neske, 1959.

HEIDEMANN, INGEBORG. "Philosophische Theorien des Spiels." *Kant-Studien,* L (1958–1959).

HEIN, HILDE. "Play as an Aesthetic Concept." *The Journal of Aesthetics and Art Criticism,* XXVII, 1 (Fall, 1968).

HEIN, PIET. *Grooks.* Cambridge, Mass.: MIT Press, 1966.

HERRICK, MARVIN T. *Comic Theory in the Sixteenth Century.* Urbana: University of Illinois Press, 1964.

HESSE, HERMANN. *Magister Ludi.* Trans. M. Savill. New York: Ungar Publishing Co., 1965.

HOPPER, STANLEY R. "The Author in Search of His Anecdote." *Restless Adventure.* Edited by Roger Shinn. New York: Charles Scribner's Sons, 1968.

———— and DAVID L. MILLER, eds. *Interpretation: The Poetry of Meaning.* New York: Harcourt, Brace and World, 1967.

HUIZINGA, JOHAN. *Homo Ludens: A Study of the Play Element in Culture.* Trans. R. F. C. Hull. Boston: Beacon Press, 1955.

JASPERS, KARL. *The Great Philosophers.* Trans. R. Mannheim. New York: Harcourt, Brace and World, 1966.

JENSEN, ADOLF. *Myth and Cult among Primitive Peoples.* Chicago: University of Chicago Press, 1963.

JONES, TOM. *The Fantasticks.* New York: Drama Book Shop, 1964.

JUNG, CARL G. *Answer to Job.* New York: The World Publishing Company, 1960.

———— . *Modern Man in Search of a Soul.* Trans. W. Dell and C. F. Baynes. New York: Harcourt, Brace and World, 1933.

———— . *Psyche and Symbol.* Edited by V. S. de Laszlo. Garden City: Doubleday and Company, 1958.

KAUFMANN, WALTER. *Critique of Religion and Philosophy.* New York: Harper & Brothers, 1958.

KERENYI, CARL. *The Religion of the Greeks and Romans.* New York: E. P. Dutton and Co., 1962.

KIERKEGAARD, SØREN. *Concluding Unscientific Postscript.* Trans. D. Swenson and W. Lowrie. Princeton: Princeton University Press, 1941.

———. *Edifying Discourses: A Selection.* New York: Harper & Row, 1958.

KOESTLER, ARTHUR. *The Act of Creation.* New York: The Macmillan Company, 1964.

KUJAWA, GERHARD. *Ursprung und Sinn des Spiels.* Cologne: E. A. Seeman Verlag, 1949.

LAO TZU. *The Way of Lao Tzu.* Trans. Wing-tsit Chan. Indianapolis: Bobbs-Merrill Co., 1963.

LARRABEE, ERIC, and ROLF MEYERSOHN, eds. *Mass Leisure.* Glencoe: The Free Press, 1958.

LAUTER, PAUL, ed. *Theories of Comedy.* Garden City: Doubleday and Company, 1964.

LEE, ROBERT. *Religion and Leisure in America.* Nashville: Abingdon Press, 1964.

LEHMAN, H. C., and P. A. WITTY. *The Psychology of Play Activities.* New York: A. S. Barnes, 1927.

LORENZ, KONRAD. *On Aggression.* Trans. M. K. Wilson. New York: Bantam Books, 1967.

LYNCH, WILLIAM. *Christ and Apollo.* New York: Sheed and Ward, 1960.

MCLUHAN, MARSHALL. *The Gutenberg Galaxy.* Toronto: University of Toronto Press, 1962.

———. *Understanding Media: The Extensions of Man.* New York: McGraw-Hill Book Co., 1965.

——— and QUENTIN FIORE. *The Medium Is the Massage.* New York: Bantam Books, 1967.

MARCUSE, HERBERT. *Eros and Civilization.* New York: Random House, 1955.

MAY, ROLLO. *Psychology and the Human Dilemma.* Princeton: D. Van Nostrand Co., 1967.

MEAD, GEORGE HERBERT. *Mind, Self, and Society.* Chicago: University of Chicago Press, 1934.

MILLAR, SUSANNA. *The Psychology of Play*. Baltimore: Penguin Books, 1968.

MONTAIGNE, MICHEL. *The Complete Essays of Montaigne*. Trans. D. Frame. Garden City: Doubleday and Company, 1960.

MORRISON, ELEANOR S. "Leisure, Worship, and Play." *Crossroads* (March, 1966).

NEALE, ROBERT. *Play and the Sacred: Toward a Theory of Religion as Play*. Ann Arbor: University Microfilms, Inc., 1964.

———. "Religion and Play." *Crossroads* (July-September, 1967).

NEUMANN, ERICH. *The Origins and History of Consciousness*. Trans. R. F. C. Hull. New York: Harper & Row, 1962.

NICHOLAS OF CUSA. *Oeuvres Choisies de Nicolas de Cues*. Trans. M. De Gandillac. Aubier: Éditions Montaigne, 1942.

———. *Philosophisch-Theologische Schriften*. Vienna: Verlag Herder, 1967.

NIETZSCHE, FRIEDRICH. "On Truth and Lie in an Extra-Moral Sense." *The Portable Nietzsche*. Edited by Walter Kaufmann. New York: Viking Press, 1954.

OLSSON, KARL A. *The God Game*. New York: The World Publishing Company, 1968.

PERRY, HENRY TEN EYCK. *Masters of Dramatic Comedy and Their Social Themes*. Cambridge, Mass.: Harvard University Press, 1939.

PIAGET, JEAN. *Play, Dreams and Imitation in Childhood*. Trans. C. Gattegno and F. M. Hodgson. New York: W. W. Norton, 1962.

PIEPER, JOSEF. *Leisure: The Basis of Culture*. Trans. A. Dru. New York: New American Library, 1963.

PIRANDELLO, LUIGI. *The Rules of the Game*. Baltimore: Penguin Books, 1959.

PLATO. *The Dialogues*. Trans. B. Jowett. Oxford: Clarendon Press, 1892.

———. *Epistles*. Trans. G. R. Morrow. Indianapolis: Bobbs-Merrill Co., 1962.

———. *Republic*. Trans. B. Jowett. New York: Random House, n.d.

POTTER, STEPHEN. *The Theory and Practice of Gamesmanship*. New York: Bantam Books, 1965.

———. *Three-Upmanship*. New York: Holt, Rinehart and Winston, 1962.

PRUYSER, PAUL. *A Dynamic Psychology of Religion*. New York: Harper & Row, 1968.

RAHNER, HUGO. *Man at Play*. Trans. B. Battershaw and E. Quinn. New York: Herder and Herder, 1967.

RAPOPORT, ANATOL. *Two-Person Game Theory: The Essential Ideas*. Ann Arbor: University of Michigan Press, 1966.

RIEFF, PHILIP. *The Triumph of the Therapeutic*. New York: Harper & Row, 1966.

RILKE, RAINER MARIA. *Duino Elegies*. Trans. C. F. MacIntyre. Berkeley: University of California Press, 1965.

———. *Sonnets to Orpheus*. Trans. C. F. MacIntyre. Berkeley: University of California Press, 1960.

SAKOL, JEANNIE. *The Inept Seducer or Bad Intentions Are Not Enough*. New York: Price, Stern, Sloan, 1968.

SCHILLER, J. C. F. *On the Aesthetic Education of Man*. Trans. R. Snell. London: Routledge and Kegan Paul, 1954.

SCHUTZ, WILLIAM C. *Joy: Expanding Human Awareness*. New York: Grove Press, 1967.

SEUSS, DR. *The Cat in the Hat Comes Back!* New York: Random House, 1958.

SHAKESPEARE, WILLIAM. *The Complete Works*. Edited by G. L. Kittredge. New York: Ginn and Co., 1936.

"SMITH, ADAM." *The Money Game*. New York: Random House, 1968.

SMITH, ROBERT PAUL. *"Where Did You Go?" "Out." "What Did You Do?" "Nothing."* New York: Pocket Books, 1959.

The Srimad-Bhagavatam. Trans. J. M. Sanyal. Calcutta: Oriental Publishing Co., 1952.

STEPHENSON, WILLIAM. *The Play Theory of Mass Communication*. Chicago: University of Chicago Press, 1967.

STERN, J. P. *Lichtenberg: A Doctrine of Scattered Occasions*. Bloomington: Indiana University Press, 1959.

STEWART, DOUGLAS J. "The Humanities, the Whore and the Alderman." *AAUP Bulletin*, LI, 1 (Autumn, 1965).

STOPPARD, TOM. *Rosencrantz and Guildenstern Are Dead*. New York: Grove Press, 1967.

SZASZ, THOMAS. *Law, Liberty and Psychiatry.* New York: Collier Books, 1968.

———. *The Myth of Mental Illness.* New York: Dell Publishing Co., 1967.

THASS-THIENEMANN, THEODORE. *The Subconscious Language.* New York: Washington Square Press, 1967.

The Upanishads. Trans. Juan Mascaro. Baltimore: Penguin Books, 1965.

VAIHINGER, HANS. *The Philosophy of "As-If."* Trans. C. K. Ogden. New York: Barnes and Noble, 1924.

VAN DER LEEUW, GERARDUS. *Sacred and Profane Beauty: The Holy in Art.* Trans. D. F. Green. New York: Holt, Rinehart and Winston, 1963.

VICO, GIAMBATTISTA. *The New Science.* Trans. J. Bergin and M. Fisch. Garden City: Doubleday and Company, 1961.

VOEGELIN, ERIC. *Order and History,* vol. 3, *Plato and Aristotle.* Baton Rouge: Louisiana State University Press, 1957.

WACH, JOACHIM. *The Comparative Study of Religions.* New York: Columbia University Press, 1961.

WATTS, ALAN. *Beyond Theology: The Art of Godmanship.* New York: Pantheon Books, 1964.

———. *The Book: On the Taboo against Knowing Who You Are.* New York: Pantheon Books, 1966.

WATZLAWICK, PAUL. "A Review of the Double-Bind Theory." *Family Process,* II, 1 (March, 1963).

WHEELWRIGHT, PHILIP. *Heraclitus.* New York: Atheneum, 1964.

WITTGENSTEIN, LUDWIG. *Philosophical Investigations.* Trans. G. E. M. Anscombe. Oxford: Blackwell, 1953.

Index of Proper Names